Patnam Subramanya Iyer
A "Beacon Light"
Among Post-Trinity Composers

Patnam Subramanya Iyer
A "Beacon Light"
Among Post-Trinity Composers

Dr. P.B. KANNA KUMAR

KANISHKA PUBLISHERS, DISTRIBUTORS
NEW DELHI-110 002

KANISHKA PUBLISHERS, DISTRIBUTORS
4697/5-21A, Ansari Road, Daryaganj
New Delhi-110 002
Phones : 2327 0497, 2328 8285
Fax : 011-2328 8285
e-mail: kanishka_publishing@yahoo.co.in

First Published 2007

ISBN 81-7391-910-0

PRINTED IN INDIA

Published by Madan Sachdeva for Kanishka Publishers, Distributors, 4697/5-21A, Ansari Road, Daryaganj, New Delhi-110 002; Typeset by Sunshine Graphics, Delhi, and Printed at Nice Printing Press, Delhi.

Foreword

Karnatic music has been justly acclaimed as a system of music with inexhaustible wealth of compositions. The compositions serve the vital purpose of retaining the structural solidarity of a system of music and this is the reason how Karnatic music has maintained an unmistakeable image of its own in the midst of various other competing systems of music. A very prominent name among composers who have made solid contribution in this regard was PATNAM SUBRAMANYA IYER who was fondly nick named as "Chinna Tyagaraja" even during the life time of the patriarch. He occupies a very special place among composers and any serious study of Karnatic music will not be complete without a proper analysis and understanding of the contribution of Sri PATNAM SUBRAMANYA IYER.

Dr. P.B. KANNA KUMAR has made an intensive research on Patnam Subramanya Iyer and has now flowered into an author of a book exclusively on the great composer. The book is sure to be of high reference value to all researchers and practioners of Karnatic music. Some rare Varnams, Kritis, Javalis and Tillana in Devanāgari and English script have been annexed to enhance the authenticity of the book. The book is a valuable addition to publications in Karnatic music.

Sangita Mahamahopadhyaya
T.R. Subramanyam
New L-17/Old L-24,
26th Street, Cauvery Colony,
Anna Nagar East,
Chennai – 600 102.

Dated: 24/7/2006

Preface

Spirituality among Indians, owes its existence to the great poets, philosophers and saint singers who have contributed to its development from time to time. In South Indian classical music i.e. Karnatic music the era of Trinity composers (Tyagaraja, Muthuswamy Dikshitar and Syamasastry) is called the Golden era, due to its unique speciality. It paved the way for further development in traditional and bhakti-oriented music. The Trinity's compositions have always reigned supreme allowing only a subordinate co-existence to the composers of future generations. At the end of the Golden era they had set impeccable standards for the rest to fallow.

After the Trinity period propagation of spirituality through music continued with the efforts of the Post-Trinity Composers, prominent among them being PATNAM SUBRAMANYA IYER, whose work is the subject of this book.

Patnam Subramanya Iyer followed the footsteps of Tyagaraja, he followed the great saint in the flow of Dhatu, Matu and structural format and also in the language chosen as medium i.e. Telugu though his mother-tongue was Tamil. He was therefore aptly called "Chinna Tyagaraja". Among the Post-Trinity Composers, he is a beacon light. Though known to be a traditionalist, he was good at innovations too. Some of his compositions such as "Raghuvamsa Sudha" in the raga Kathanakuthuhalam which resembles Western music, are very popular even today.

It gives me immense pleasure to write about this great composer and have tried to cover as many Varnams, Kritis, Javalis and Tillanas as possible. I hope that this work would be a very valuable for students, musicians, teachers and all music lovers. However, I would like to mention that this valuable work would not have been possible without the encouragement and full support of Sangeeta Mahamahopadhyaya Vidwan Sri T.R. SUBRAMANYAM.

I would also like to thank Dr. RADHA VENKATACHALAM, Professor in Karnatic Music, Department of Music, University of Delhi for her valuable suggestions. I also acknowledge the help of my students and friends in bringing out this book.

Last but not least I owe my acknowledgements to the Kanishka Publishers and Distributors, New Delhi, who undertook the printing assignment and completed the book within a short period. I have included some less known Varnams in Adi and Ata Talas with notation for the benefit of students and musicians with Roman and Devanagari Script. Usage of Diacritical marks have not been strictly followed. Only popular usage of spellings are used even in Kritis and other compositions.

Contents

1
Biography

Compeer of the well-known Maha Vaidyanatha Iyer, Patnam Subramanya Iyer too belonged to the sishya-parampara of Tyagaraja. The prefix, patnam, refers to the city of Madras, where he had settled and lived for about twelve years in the latter part of his glorious career. As a musician with a majestic style of his own, he was treated with great respect, on par with Maha Vaidyanatha Iyer. As a composer he was even better known, and earned the name "Chinna Tyagaraja" (Junior Tyagaraja) in his own time.

Born in 1845 in a Tamil Ashtasahasram family of Tanjore district, Patnam Subramanya Iyer inherited his musical talents from his ancestors. His grandfather, Bharatam Panchanada Sastri, was among the Asthana Vidvans of Serfoji Maharaja of Tanjore. His father, Bharatam Vaidyanatha Iyer, also was a musician and scholar. It was his uncle, Melattur Ganapathi Sastri, who initiated him into music. Later, he studied under Manambuchavadi Venkatasubbayyar, a distinguished pupil of Tyagaraja and Guru of Maha Vaidyanatha Iyer, Sarabha Sastri and others.

Patnam Subramanya Iyer was not gifted with a naturally mellifluous voice. He, therefore, put in rigorous practice and cultivated his rather unimpressive voice into a highly mobile and musical one. He was equally at home in the slow and in the fast tempos. While still in his early thirties he became a very famous musician sought after by Maharajās, Zamindaṛs and Mirasdars̄s. He was among the very few musicians who received annual honoraria from a number of Samasthanaṃs like Mysore, Travancoṛe, Vizianagaram and Ramanathapuram.

Begada was his favourite raga, which he is said to have sung for days together. He, therefore, came to be known as Begada Subramanya Iyer also. He was an adept par excellence in Tala and he composed and sang a Pallavi in Simhanandanam, the longeṣt of the talas.

He was held in high esteem by his contemporaries like Maha Vaidyanatha Iyer and Tirukkodikaval Krishna Iyer, the great violinist. The latter often accompanied him in his concerts. His residence used to be frequented by many distinguished admirers like Panditturai Tevar, Zamindar of Palavanattam. It was Panditturai who requested Patnam subramanya Iyer to teach Poochchi Srinivasa Iyengar.

Maha Vaidyanatha Iyer and Patnam Subramanya Iyer were quite friendly, they having lived on the east and on the west side of the great temple at Tiruvaiyaru. However, the admirers of the two Vidvaṇs sometimes took a partism view and indulged in uncomplimentary remarks against the principals. Maha Vaidyanatha Iyer's own brother Ramaswami Sivan erred in this way, in a book he published after the death of his brother. It resulted in the publication of a protest (Khandanam) by Patnam Subramanya Iyer, and then a counter-protest from Vina Vaidyanatha Iyer. Rather unfortunate.

For many years Subramanya Iyer shone as a leading Lakshya-Lakshana Vidvan. He also composed a number of compositions of his own. Coming of Tyagaraja's lineage he naturally chose the former's style. Some of his kritīs cannot be easily distinguished from Tyagaraja's. He was one of the many Tamil composers who composed in Telugu in preference to their own mother tongue. This was possibly because of the influence of Tyagaraja's compositions. Some of his compositions, are in Sanskrit. He has to his credit about hundred compositions, mainly kritīs. Other forms include Tana Varnams̄, Pada Varnams̄, Javalīs and Tillanās. They are all in the popular talās. "Paridanamichchite" in Bilhari, "Marivere Dikkevarayya" in Shanmukhapriya, "Ninnujuchi" in Sourashtram are among his well-known compositions. The raga Kadanakutuhalam was his creation, crystallized in his famous "Raghuvamsa Sudhambudhi" wherein his mastery in composing chittasvaram is also evident. The raga, perhaps composed for a foreign dignitary in a royal court, has touches of European music. The mudra (signature) he used was "Venkatesa" or "Venkateswara", simply or prefixed by Sri or Adi or Varada. There are other composers who have used this same mudra.

Another distinction of Patnam Subramanya Iyer was his illustrious list of pupils, some of them equally well-known composers. Among them were Ramanathapuram Poochchi Srinivasa Iyengar, Mysore Vasudevachar and "Tiger" Varadachariar. There were also women pupils who learnt from him, like Enadi Sisters and Salem Meenakshi's daughters. It was to facilitate the teaching of some of his pupils that he settled down at Madras. His residence at Madras, and that of another great musician-composer, Tyagayyar, son of Vina Kuppayyar (disciple of Tyagaraja) at Tiruvottiyur near Madras exerted a major influence on the cultural flowering of the city into the great seat of musical patronage that it is today.

Patnam Subramanya Iyer had no children and, therefore, adopted his sister's grandson. In his last days he had moved back to Tiruvaiyaru and he passed away there on 31st July 1902. His name will live long through his musical compositions.

❋❋❋

2

State of Carnatic Music during Patnam Subramanya Iyer's Time

History of mankind has been bisected into two major chunks as B.C. and A.D. The period denoted by B.C. is the one before the advent of Jesus Christ and A.D. the period after him. While this is the major and widely accepted method of reckoning historical time, there are other methods in chronology of time like Salivahana Sahabda, Quilon years of Kerala in our country. There is a similar phenomenon with reference to Prophet Mohammed also, followed in some Muslim countries of the world. In all these systems the bifurcation point is always associated with a prominent personality like Jesus Christ, Emperor Salivahna, Vikramaditya or Prophet. These personalities were responsible for major changes in the world around them in such measure that the world before and after them was so different as to be considered as of different eras.

In the history of music one such major period of renaissance was brought about by Tyagaraja and his illustrious contemporaries Dikshitar and Syama Sastri, called popularly as the musical Trinity. The whole of Carnatic Music world was not what it was after the period of these Trinity. Students of music are thus able to study history under two distinctive periods pre-Trinity and post-Trinity. Lot more has happened to the art of music in the two centuries of the Trinity and post-Trinity era than in the many centuries of the pre-Trinity period.

Before advent of the Trinity, classical music does not seem to have been finding a place in the main stream of the life of the common man. Classical music was being sung, played, heard and appreciated only in small pockets here and there, mostly in the courts and harems of kings, chieftains and other wealthy people. Only folk music was commonly prevalent among the people and classical music and musicians were being given respect not necessarily out of knowledgeable appreciation but more because of the pious and learned image of classical musicians that was current in those days. There was generally an undue restraint in the dissemination of the knowledge of classical music which was over-mystified as something celestial, meant only for the elite and the upper classes and not to a commoner. The form and shape of classical music was liquid and not lucid until the time of the Trinity and this lack of concreteness came in the way of its finding a distinct place in the day-to-day life of people.

The kriti form was consolidated and fully established only at the time of and by the Trinity. Emergence of the kriti form is a major landmark in the history of classical music. The kriti is the staple-food for classicism. Its main purpose is to contain and preserve the essence of the ragas which are by themselves rather too abstract for a common man to identify and enjoy. But when a raga is encased in the kriti which has the catchyness of the rhythm and easier assimilation because of the lyric that is employed with adherence to rules of prosody and metre, it is brought within easier reach of even the less initiated mortals. Compositions prior to the days of the Trinity did not have the solid shape, authentic tune and the classical weight of the kritis of the Trinity. It is said that Purandara Dasa composed 4,75,000 compositions but it is difficult to understand how all these songs could have been sung in those days when the number of ragas prevalent could not have been more than a hundred. Judged from that level of having to accommodate lakhs of songs in mere hundreds of tunes, the period of the Trinity can very well be called one of Himalayan growth.

The total number of available compositions of the Trinity might hardly be two thousand but their contribution to the growth of classical music is many thousands of times more than that of all pre-Trinity compositions mainly because each and every composition of the Trinity is couched in a tune of its own, distinctly different from one another. A lot of classical music has been capsuled in the kritis of the Trinity and this stock seems to be able to last for all centuries to come. The course of history of music can thus be said to have entered into a new world of large proportions not known hitherto. The bifurcation of musical history into pre and post-Trinity periods is thus fully justified.

Composers can also be studied and analysed with reference to their period, pre-Trinity or post-Trinity. Post-Trinity composers had the great advantage of the impeccable models and standards set by the Trinity. It was enough for them if they could closely follow the foot-steps of the three illustrious predecessors. Of the three, Tyagaraja naturally had a much larger following. It is worthwhile discussing the reasons why Tyagaraja had the maximum number of not only listeners and students but also composers that chose to trail his path. Though all the three Trinitarians had preservation and propagation of classical music in the background of Bhakti as their mission in life, only Tyagaraja among them would seem to particularly care for the common man and reach classical music to the people at large. His Lingua Franca was Telugu which he could couch in easily understandable music with a catchy rhythmic structure. Dikshitar's compositions were almost entirely in Sanskrit that is not a spoken language and so not within easy reach of the common man. Though Syama Sastry employed only Telugu as his medium, his penchent for experiments in laya and talas made it rather difficult for an uninitiated person to easily grasp, enjoy and follow his style. Tyagaraja on the other hand took pains to invent a catchy new Eduppu like 'half of the little finger' which made even the less gifted learners sing these songs with some confidence and technical correctness. For instance the number of listeners who can sing a "Sarasa Sāma Dāna" or "Marugēlara" with condifence is sure to be much more than those trying to master a song like "Dakshinamūrthe" (Sankarabharanam) or a "Māyamma" (Ahiri). This does not mean that Dikshitar and Syama Sastry were deliberately composing at a level above the reach of an average student. Their approach to the whole situations seems to have been conditioned by various factors like Srividya Upasana, incorporation of technical excellence and embellishments like Raga Mudra, Kshetra Varnanam and the like. But Tyagaraja chose to sing mainly about Lord Rāma, who was and is easily the most widely followed Godhead. More people certainly know the story of Rāma than about Devi and other Gods and Godessess. Thus Tyagaraja has employed the most familiar themes in equally familiar language in a music and rhythm that is readily assimilable to the common man and no wonder he has the maximum number of emulaters.

The period of Patnam Subramanya Iyer can thus be said to be one that was conducive to a creative mind to progress. The path established by the Trinity was there for all to follow and this was both an advantage and a challenge too. While many could have made bold to compose songs in the pattern established by Tyagaraja, his image was too big for any other subsequent composer to hope to outshine. The Trinity's compositions continue to reign supreme till today allowing only a subordinate co-existence to a few of the composers of the succeeding generations. Among such composers Patnam Subramanya Iyer was easily on the top, richly deserving the title "Chinna Tyagaraja".

The environment during Patnam Subramanya Iyer's days was also favourably different from the earlier days. The circle of people with interest or atleast a curiosity for classical music had enlarged, thanks to the contribution of the Trinity. More members of the aristocracy were now interested in associations with musicians at least as a status symbol, if not out of genuine interest or knowledge in music. Musicians had comparatively more occasions to sing before an audience and exhibit their talent. There were infact talent contests among musicians sponsored by the various patrons. Such contests have vanished today. The contests did have some contribution to make. It encouraged the contestants to be alert all the time, adding to one's equipment and knowledge in music, to be able to outwit and outdo the opponent. Striving for excellence was thus a way of life in those days for any musician who wanted to be in the vanguard. Specialization rather than popular generalization was the need and choice of the musicians of those days and the art of classical music got all the nourishment in that environment.

The institution of platform concerts had also begun to emerge during Patnam Subramanya Iyer's days. Such concerts were in addition to the sittings in Palaces and contests. The former type of concerts were different both in the form and content. The audience in public concerts were people at large with multifarious tastes and levels of knowledge and were larger in number too. To cater to such an audience, the musicians cannot just exhibit their specializations of any particular branch of music but must be able to first entertain the masses with a befitting stuff. In other words a platform musician was not free to sing what he wanted but must be prepared to sing what the listeners wanted. An average listener was generally fascinated by variety rather than virtuosity. More number of items within the duration of the concert was more welcome to him than singing one Ragam-Tanam-Pallavi extensively for two hours. Such elaborate singing was, on the other hand, looked for in chamber concerts in Palaces or in contests. Of these two types of platforms the glamour of catching the attention of large number of people was possible only in public sabha concerts and the demand of this platform was not so much on the creative ability of the musician as on a clever and neat presentation of rehearsed or crammed stuff. The kritis thus gained the upper hand and usurped the pride of place from pallavis. By that time the kritis of the Trinity, particularly Tyagaraja, were handily available and the time allotted for Manodharma Sangeeta was encroached upon. What started like this about a century ago has developed to an unduly large extent today, the result being that the art of Ragam-

Tanam-Pallavi is veritably facing extinction and kritis have proliferated like anything.

Patnam Subramanya Iyer flourished at this juncture when the importance and demand for specializations in rendering of kritis was beginning, eclipsing the grandeur of Ragam-Tanam-Pallavi singing. The situation was one in which there was a tendency and encouragement to compose more and more of Kritis. In those days, however, pallavi singing was still kept in good esteem though it was no longer enjoying the monopoly it had in the earlier days.

There was one more reason too for musicians to dabble in composing. The chances of a person's name remembered after his time are much more if he had been a composer. If even one or two of his compositions had proved popular, he is sure to be remembered by atleast a few generations after him. There are instances of composer's names having been perpetuated by virtue of just a single composition. Prominent examples: Pachchimiriyam Adiyappayya whose only widely popular "Viriboni" varnam (Bhairavi) has immortalized his name. The popular song "Sringaralahari" in Neelambari by Mysore Lingaraj is another case in point. These composers might have composed many other songs which have not gained currency but a single composition of them clicking in the field has been enough to remind their names to posterity. More than composing, writing a book is a more effective means of perpetuating the name of the author. A mere eminent performing artist will remain celebrated only during his life time that too mainly during the peak period of his career. But his name is very likely to be forgotten within the course of a few generations. But in the case of a composer, his songs will keep the people reminded of him for a much longer future. The period of rememberance is further longer for authors of works. All of us know the name of Bharata today, 2000 years after his time, because his book "Natyasastra" has survived all these centuries. But do we know the name of any great singer of the fourth century B.C. today? There must have been famous musicians in all the centuries but majority of the names familiar to us today are all like Jayadeva, Nārayanateertha, Annamācharya, Sāranga Deva, Ramamatya, Venkatamukhi etc., who were all either composers or authors.

It is human nature to long for fame not only during one's life time but also to have one's name perpetuated into the future and composing songs or writing books helps to achieve this more than remaining a mere performing artist. No wonder, therefore, that many a musician tried his or her hand into the art of composing and those who cannot sing at all tried to get some book or other of theirs into print. All may like to have eternal fame but only a few could have the requisite merit for the same. It is worth-while noticing here that all written works of musicology belonging to the period from pre-Christian era to the end of 20th century are not necessarily of high practical value. Similarly, the number of composers has of late grown to a large extent. There are more composers than singers today and the field is flooded with compositions.

But there have been good composers too who have genuinely contributed to the growth of classical music without just numerically adding to the stock of existing compositions. The Trinity had the most justifiable and laudable mission of composing kirits that would preserve classical values for posterity. But for the Trinity, classical music would not be in the high pedestel in which it is today. The main purpose of any composition, particularly the kriti, is to serve as a perennial store house of at least one particular phase of a raga. Any composer is justified if his composition aims to cover and contain a new facet of a traditional raga or a new raga itself. A composer might sometimes be prompted to sing the praise of a particular deity in the form of a musical composition but even then his effort would be of real worth only if there is some musical richness also in it. Expertise in literary poetry is a gift different from that in composing a kriti and the grammatical demands on the two are also not identical. We may thus have a very able creative musician with not a matchingly high gift in poesy or also a person of rich literary vocabulary not knowing any music at all. In a good composer, these two virtues must blend in an optimum proportion. One such rare composer was Patnam Subramanya Iyer.

He lived at a period conducive for a musician to freely move ahead in all branches of the art of music, be it learning, performing, composing or teaching. Classical music had by then gained enough currency in society, encouraging more number of people to try learning music. Patnam Subramanya Iyer had the great advantage of musical ancestry and he had quality training in music unasked. He had as his guru the veteran Manambuchavadi Venkata Subbayyar who was a relative and a senior disciple of Tyagaraja himself. Because of the advent of the institutions that arranged public music concerts, Patnam Subramanya Iyer and his contemporaries had more number of opportunities to perform before varied audience while still having the other venues like the king's courts, temple festivals and marriages. What to sing in a concert was not a problem since the kritis of Tyagaraja were handy and audience were generally attending concerts with awe and reverence unlike today's listeners whose attitude is disgustingly casual or even condescending. The Trinity had also paved a royal road and sterling models for the art of composing. Another source of enlarging knowledge was through teaching students of good caliber. Patnam Subramanya Iyer had all of such healthy environment and he naturally flowered into a famous musician, respected composer, venerated guru — all in one.

❋ ❋ ❋

3

Patnam Subramanya Iyer's Contribution Tyagaraja's Influence

It is as if by divine dispensation that in the two centuries 18th and 19th—the field of classical music was given an uplift and facelift not only in India but also in other parts of the world like European Countries. Great composers like Beethoven flourished in Europe at that time when we had the Trinity here. The compositions of the Trinity did the great service of making classical music intelligible to the common man. The Trinity's contribution has been very vast, great, deep and sublime. Qualitatively their work is of Himalayan height and all time greatness and quantitatively too they have left behind an inexhaustively rich legacy. The varieties of kritis and other types of compositions pioneered by them remains unexcelled even today, nearly two centuries after that time. From a near vaccum of the pre-Trinity days to a veritable flood of solid classical compositions available in the post-Trinity days has indeed been a miraculous metamorphosis for the music world and the successive generations could unendingly draw from the gift of the Trinity, who would seem to have exhausted all possibilities in the field of compositions. To the generations closely succeeding the Trinity, this situation was both an advantage and a handicap. It was advantage in the sense that the composers of that period need not grope in the dark while attempting to create a new song and can very easily and safely beat the strong track paved by the immediate predecessors, the Trinity. The very urge to compose a song was not considered anything unnatural since Trinity had made the world understand the value of kritis and their kritis were striking models for all other composers to emulate. Their models are infact still reigning supreme and nothing more effective has so far been invented by any subsequent composer in the format of classical composition. The Trinity's model was thus a great advantage but it was also a challenge to the new entrants in the field. The impact of the Trinity's kritis was so great that it must have been a herculean task for the later composers to make any name. The standard established by the Trinity was so high that the successors were considered to have achieved enough even if their compositions were mere faithful attempts in the same path. Apart from sheer excellence of their creations the Trinity lead lives of such austerity and renunciation that they were legends in their own life time and such a spiritual status could not be attained by composers of the succeeding generations. The post-Trinity Composers did not find places in the list of great Bhaktās or ascetics. Because he embraced Sanyāsa Āshram towards the end of his life, Tyagaraja is called "Tyagaraja Swamy" and Dikshitar was a venerated Devi Upasaka. So was Syama Sastry who was hailed as one possessing anugraha and nigraha shakti, i.e. the verbal power to curse or cure. Such an image of this Trinity was far above what can be expected in an average human being, however, talented he may be in music. That a composer should be a human being with super human capabilities was thus sort of a norm made prevalent and to rise to this level not only in music but also in spirituality was too difficult a task for the post-Trinity Composers. As if influenced by this set of values composers like Maha Vaidyanatha Sivan took pains to project an image of themselves as Siva Bhaktās in addition to being adepts in the art. At least in strictly observing religious rituals the musicians of those days had to be and were very particular so that they might be able to claim to at least remotely belong to the clan of composers like the Trinity. To maintain even that level should have been difficult in that period in which the commercial element in the music field had already surfaced and music was shaping more as a viable profession and not a means for salvation. Such was a handicap in no small measure that the post-Trinity composers had to face and no wonder even the best among them was at best reckoned only as a miniature version of the Trinity. This is how Patnam Subramanya Iyer was known as only a "Chinna Tyagaraja" (a miniature version of Tyagaraja) in spite of his great level of achievement both as a performer and composer. To have remained faithful to the style of Tyagaraja and have composed kritis very much as Tyagaraja's was itself adjudged as very great.

With the passing of time between Tyagaraja and Patnam Subramanya Iyer the level of heaviness associated with classical music might have undergone a little further dilution with introduction of more of speed and catchyness. Among the Trinity it was Tyagaraja who would seem to have felt the need for such a compromise for the sake of making classical music intelligible to the common man. The demand of the people at large to ask for more of this is understandable. But Tyagaraja and his followers were still very much within the classicial frame, modifying it only in the makeup to suit the times. It is also quite natural that Patnam Subramanya Iyer who belonged to the Tyagaraja's dynasty, wanted to stick to that school and in his innate humility he felt that he could at best only emulate and never excel the great patriarch. He has thus faithfully carried forward the pattern of Madhyamakala kritis, particularly those starting in half of the little finger, an Eduppu invented and popularised by Tyagaraja (there is no kriti of Dikshitar or Syama Sastry in this Eduppu). "Marivere" (Shanmukhapriya) "Aparādhamu" (Latangi) "Raghuvamsa" (Kathanakutuhalam), "Ninnu Jeppa" (Mandari) are shining examples of this pattern.

Patnam Subramanya Iyer's mother tongue was Tamil but he did not compose even a single song in that language. His choosing Telugu as a Lingua France need not have been for the reason that he found it superior to Tamil or his command over the former was so high. It might have been because of the indelible influence of Tyagaraja whom he wanted to faithfully follow not only in the flow of Dhatu and structural format but also in each and every other detail including the languages chosen as medium. Besides Telugu Tyagaraja has employed Sanskrit for some of the kritis. The pancharatna kriti in Nāta is a classic show-window of Tyagaraja's command in Sanskrit. In majority of the kritis, however, Tyagaraja has employed only Sanskritized Telugu unlike Kshetragna. Patnam Subramanya Iyer's choice has also been identical. He has also handled only Sanskrit and Telugu and no other language, even his own mother tongue. The level of Sanskritization in Patnam Subramanya Iyer's compositions is not that much as in Tyagaraja's and in this area he can be said to have scored a little higher than the latter. Perhaps because of his limited number of compositions Patnam Subramanya Iyer could manage without much of mixture of languages. In his prolific output of compositions Tyagaraja has at times gone about with odd mixture of words of Telugu and Sanskrit. For example, 'Māmava Raghu Rāma' (Sāranga) in the last charanam

> Rājādhipa Tyāga-
> rājavinuta – Bāga (Māmava)

The Telugu word 'Bāga' has been prefixed with the Sanskrit word 'Māmava'. Asking to be protected well is never expressed with the words Bāga-Māmava in either Sanskrit or Telugu. The ending of 'Tyāga' and 'Bāga' in the two lines and 'Rāga' and 'Rāja' as the opening words in the lines is euphoniously and prosodically appealing and to accommodate this, Tyagaraja does not seem to have minded the odd combination of words like Bāga-Māmava. Peccadillos like these are not wanting in Tyagaraja and these are almost totally absent in Kshetragna and also in Patnam Subramanya Iyer. Kshetragna was a native of Andhra who lived major part of his life in Andhra Pradesh. He could 'think' in Telugu and give expression in a natural flow of that language. Though the mother tongue of Tyagaraja was Telugu, he was born and brought up entirely in Tamil Nadu and he grew in an environment where the use of Telugu was rather Tamilized and the influence of this is seen in his kritis.

To Patnam Subramanya Iyer, Telugu was an alien language. He had to 'think' first in Tamil and then search for words in Telugu to express his thoughts. This sort of contrived expression makes the Telugu of Patnam Subramanya Iyer sound different from that of a Bhadrāchala Rāmadāsa or Kshetragna who could go about in Telugu as the duck taking to water. There must be a difference between a duck and an ace swimmer in their movements in water and Patnam Subramanya Iyer's dealing with Telugu can be compared to the latter. Though Telugu was not his mother tongue, he seems to have taken pains to build-up enough vocabulary for purposes of composing songs. His Telugu would, therefore, be grammatically correct though not of a natural flow that could be expected in an Andhra. Patnam Subramanya Iyer will easily rank very high among non-Andhra Composers, many of whom are not free from grammatical inaccuracies in the sāhityam. This lapse is not because of their ignorance or incapacity but only out of their lack of touch with the idiom of that language. For instance, Poochchi Srinivasa Iyengar whose mother tongue was Tamil has composed that brilliant song "Saraguna Pālimpa" (Kedaragaula) which is easily one of the best pieces in that raga. In the first line of the charanam he has used the word 'Gaja Rājudu', obviously taking it in the stride as 'Rāmudu' and 'Krishnudu'. He seems to have over-looked the fact that in Telugu language the process of declention is not the same for the words 'Rāma' and 'Rāju'. This small inaccuracy need not, however, come in the way of any student of music in learning and being benefited by 'Saraguna Pālimpa' which is like a touch stone for Kedaragaula. Patnam Subramanya Iyer is almost totally free from such pitfalls though a certain amount of lack of naturalness in flow of Telugu in his compositions is noticeable.

In kritis like 'Inta Kante Kāvalena I Kashtamu Chālada' Patnam Subramanya Iyer seems to have taken recourse to rather too earthy a language looking like prose. Similar passages occur in other kritis, exampled below:

1. 'Karunincha' (Husseni)
   Anupallavi: Nannu Parulevvado yani Yenchaka.

2. 'Neeve Gatiyani' (Purnachandrika)
   Charanam: Sthiramuga Sri Venkateswarudu Balkinadi Telusu konti.
3. 'Manasu Karuga' (Hamsadhwani)
   Charanam: Saranamanina Degakai Tana Sareeramunu Kōsi Ichchina.
   (Dega means Eagle; In the episode referred to it was not the Eagle but only the Pigeon that asked for sarana).
4. 'Endukitu Chapalamu' (Mandari)
5. 'Ittivāruletiki Puttenayya' (Ramapriya)

The language used in these kritis is not subtle but rather too open.

The discussion on the compositions of any composer will not be complete with an analysis of the sāhitya only. We shall, therefore, look at the Dhātu portion of Patnam Subramanya Iyer's contribution. Because of his commitment to the path of Tyagaraja, Patnam Subramanya Iyer has also paid more attention to Madhyamakāla and majority of his kritis are in single kalai. The better known double kalai kritis of his are 'Nija Dāsa Varada' (Kalyani) and 'Inka Daya' (Chakravakam); Ninnu Juchi' (Sourashtram) is being sung in double kalai by some and in single kalai by others. 'Nijadāsa Varada' can not be said to be among the best kritis in Kalyani. The level of excellence reached in single kalai kritis of Patnam Subramanya Iyer is higher than what is found in double kalai kritis. The concept of introducing sangatis had become well established by the time of Patnam Subramanya Iyer whose kritis give lot of scope for sangatis. The set of sangatis prominent in 'Ninnu Juchi' (Sourashtram) and 'Nijadāsa Varada' (Kalyani) is ample proof of Patnam Subramanya Iyer's expertise in this area.

There does not seem to be any definite pattern in the choice of ragas. Patnam Subramanya Iyer seems to have felt like dealing with Todi, Kambhoji and Sankarabharanam only in varnams. One full varnam has been allotted to Todi (Ēra Napai) while Kambhoji and Sankarabharanam occur only as part of the 'Navaragamalika Varnam' (Valachi Vachchi). Closely succeeding the Trinity has been a handicap to composers like Patnam Subramanya Iyer who must have found almost all the rakti ragas exhaustively explored and exploited by the former. Patnam Subramanya Iyer who has not exhausted all the rakti ragas has somehow had a fancy for less known ragas like Nārāyani, Mālavi, Suddha Bangala and Mandari which have all been unearthed and brought into vogue by Tyagaraja. He has infact attempted two songs in Mandari 'Ninnu Jeppa' in Adi tala and 'Yendukitu Chapalamu' in Misra chapu. It can be said that these two kritis of Patnam Subramanya Iyer in Mandari have not lifted the raga to any higher status from 'Paraloka Bhaya' of Tyagaraja. The Dhātu of the anupallavi of 'Ninnu Jeppa' is very much like that of 'Paraloka Bhaya'. The Misra chapu tempo of 'Yendukitu' does not seem to go well with Mandari raga. But in Purnachandrika 'Nejesina' Patnam Subramanya Iyer has been able to bring out newer facets of the raga not covered by Tyagaraja. So is the case with Narayani. Balahamsa must have been a well known raga upto the period of Patnam Subramanya Iyer who has given us 'Yennadu Daya Vachchuno'. Apart from the still rarer Sindhu Mandari (Karuninchuta) Patnam Subramanya Iyer has also conceived a totally new raga Kathana Kuthūhalam which remains the hot favourite with instrumentalists even today. This kriti is also entirely in Sanskrit.

Though Patnam Subramanya Iyer has been a faithful and devoted follower of Tyagaraja he has not hesitated to compose Varnams, Javalis and Tillanas which were not attempted as such by the latter. Tyagaraja is even said to have been against composing erotic songs like javalis though some of the songs in Nowka Charitram are in the javali strain which can, however, be explained as necessary evils in an operatic attempt, particularly, when the theme was of Lord Krishna and Gopis. Javalis demand more of native and colloquial language which may not come naturally to a composer with a different mother tongue and Patnam Subramanya Iyer's javalis betray this fact, as may be seen from certain portions in Mariyāda Teliyakane (Surati). He is said to have had a heavy and gruffy voice but he seems to have concentrated on single kalai kritis. It is not known whether he was singing his own compositions in his concerts but he must have been able to produce a rich effect by singing single kalai kritis in his heavy voice. He enjoyed the title "Begada Subramanya Iyer" and justifying that title has given us a very good kriti "Manasuna Nera Nammiti' and a varnam "Marachetlu" Ata tala, soaked in Begada raga bhava. When a good composer is renowned musician also the impact that he could leave on people of his own and the succeeding generations is indeed strong. He was also not free from occasional surfacing of professional pettiness. The rivalry and ribaldry that existed between him and his illustrious contemporary Maha Vaidyanatha Sivan, would make a study of their biographies saucy and interesting. Patnam Subramanya Iyer is thus an epoch-maker whose posterity has not yet chosen to deify. Though he was a confirmed traditionalist he has not hesitated to innovate and invent. Kadanakuthuhalam, a raga that would sound close to western music was his creation and his kriti 'Raghuvamsa Sudha' with its sprightly chittasvaram continues to be the hot favourite with instrumentalists for so many decades now. He is also said to have composed a humorous and remorseful song upon snuff powder and his addiction to it. One manipravāla javali with English words is also attributed to him. Patnam Subramanya Iyer has thus shown to posterity that sticking to tradition does not mean a closed mind and innovations and experiments developed upon a strong classical base is a welcome step towards progress.

TYPES OF COMPOSITIONS

Patnam Subramanya Iyer has chosen to be apart from Tyagaraja in the matter of choice in the types of compositions. Tyagaraja can be said to have confined himself to only kritis and keertanas. According to one version, Tyagaraja did not allow his disciples to pay any attention to Sringara oriented songs or arts. He is said to have chided some of his disciples when he heard them discussing a dance show witnessed by them. But the same Tyagaraja has chosen to create the Nowka Charitram which deals with the dealings the Gopis had with Krishna. Songs like 'Sringarinchukoni Vedaliri' (Surati) and 'Ōdanu Jaripe Muchchata' (Saranga) describe the pranks of the Gopis and their Lord in such detail that there is as much if not more of Sringara expected in a javali or padam. One possible excuse is that the theme of the opera demanded it and since Lord Krishna himself was the hero, it was only sublime Sringara and not any lewd poetry. It should be noted here that even in the 12th century poet, Jaya Deva has handled the Krishna and Radha theme much more openly, occasionally bordering on obscenity. Compared to Jaya Deva's Gita Govindam, Tyagaraja's Nowka Charitam can very easily be rated as much more sober and restrained in the handling of

Sringara rasa. Also, in the other opera Prahlada Bhakti Vijayam Tyagaraja has stood up to his reputation as a devotional purists and the whole work deals only with Prahalada's unlimited devotional attachment to Lord Vishnu.

By the days of Patnam Subramanya Iyer the convention that a composer should be of saintly disposition must have eased a little and so he must have thought of composing javalis and varnams too besides kritis. Varnams had made their appearance even during Tyagaraja's days but somehow the few lines of sahitya in them were all in Sringara rasa as a convention. It is said that Tyagaraja composed the Pancharatna kritis as an alternative to varnams, the conventional Sringara Sahitya of which he might have wanted to avoid.

Majority of the composers prior to the Trinity have somehow confined to only one type of composition. Thus, Jaya Deva composed only the Astapadis. Arunagirinadhar stuck to only the Tiruppugazhl format, Kshetragna only to padams, and Bhadrāchala Rāmdas to Keertanas. The quest for variety in compositions seems to have come into vogue only around the Trinity era, and by the time of the post-Trinity composers it had become common for one and the same composer attempting more than one variety of composition. Patnam Subramanya Iyer has thus chosen to compose varnams and javalis which were eschewed by Tyagaraja. It was not out of any disregard for the latter but only to conform to the contemporary practices.

Thanks to Tyagaraja, the number of people wanting to learn music and the number of serious listeners of the music had proliferated in the 19th century and the institution of

Sangeeta Sabhas had also started growing, resulting in the musician having to give more number of concerts than what their predecessors did. The platform concerts were outlets for a variety of compositions though Ragam-Tanam-Pallavi was still the piece-de-resistance. The situation today is indeed facing an over growth in the proliferation of concerts and compositions resulting in too casual an attitude in the listeners. Javalis were welcome items in the post-pallavi portion of concerts, and composers were justified in attempting javalis. The situation seems to have reached a peak during the days of Dharmapuri Subbarayar (born 1864) who composed only javalis and not any other item. Pattabhi Ramayya was another such composer. Patnam Subramanya Iyer might have felt like attempting javalis which had come into the main stream of musical repertoire in his days.

Besides Javalis, varnams had also been brought to popular vogue in the post-Trinity days. Varnams have multiple uses. They serve as store houses for preserving the grammatical accuracy of ragas. The composer of a varnam should be a Lakshana-Lakshya Vidvan of a high level of creative talent. Musicians and students of subsequent generation must be able to draw direction from varnams which should be replete with raga-bhava and also indicate the Visesha Sancharas, Apurva Prayogas, and the idiom of respective ragas. By virtue of the swara passages in them the varnams can give more specific information than the kritis about ragas. They are thus compositions of everlasting value. The varnams also occupy a very important place in the learning process of Carnatic music. They are taught and learnt with even more attention and seriousness than the kritis. Unlike kritis they are practiced in two and three degrees of speed and even in Tisra gati, necessitating a large number of repetition. Apart from being such an important composition for learners the varnams found a prominent place in the concert repertoire too as the very opening piece. Since violinists would also have learned all the popular varnams and mridangists would also have enough knowledge of the musical structure of them, the varnams are safe compositions to start a concert with, because of the assured support from the accompanists. Varnams also help the vocalist to warm up and it thus became a convention to start the concerts with a varnam.

Patnam Subramanya Iyer had all the equipments needed for composing varnams. He was a reputed performer and he had a strong grip with the classical idiom. It is but natural that a vidvan like him should have an urge to compose varnams that called for a very high degree of expertise in music and show his mettle.

Another strange aspect about varnams is that the sahityam was conventionally of a amorous nature. But the music of the varnam is such that, with the elongation of the vowel, the sahitya gets distorted and becomes undecipherable. One wonders why should a composer stick to sringara sahitya when, afterall the sahitya is not going to be heard clearly during rendition of the varnam. It is possible that Pada Varnam which had the purpose of providing accompanying music to dance had the sringara theme and Tana Varnams blindly followed that convention. That the sahityam of varnams should be dealing with sringara might have been a reason for Tyagaraja to have avoided composing varnams and chosen the Pancharatna Kritis as a substitute. Employing the sringara rasa sahitya was not such a big taboo during Patnam Subramanya Iyer's days, and the creative urge in him must have prompted him to compose varnams though his patriarch had shunned them.

PATNAM SUBRAMANYA IYER'S MUDRA

It is widely known that Patnam Subramanya Iyer used 'Venkatesa' as his Mudra. The word has been used as 'Venkateswara' in some kritis (Ninnu Jūchi-Sourashtram). 'Varada Venkateswara' and 'Adi Venkateswara' (Yetu Nammināvo-Saveri, Paridanamichchite-Bilahari) were the other variations in his Mudra. Even as he chose Telugu obviously out of inspiration from Tyagaraja, his choice of Mudra too has been influenced by his Guru Manambuchavadi Venkata Subbayyar who also used 'Venkatesa' as his signature. To the latter, it was the Swanāma Mudra and we can say it was Guru Nāma Mudra for Patnam Subramanya Iyer. But this 'Venkatesa' is rather too common place a word and other composers like Kothavasal Venkata Rāmayyar have also used the same as the mudra. Example: 'Sarasuda' Varnam-Adi tala (Saveri ragam). Some centuries earlier to this the Tāllapakam composers, Annamācharya and his associates had also the same 'Venkateswara' as the mudra. Because of the confusion created by the same mudra being used by more than one composer, some kritis are attributed to wrong authors. Some musicians feel that the 'Dhanyudevvado' (Malayamarutam) is a composition of Manambuchavadi Venkatasubbayyar but it is popularly listed under the kritis of Patnam Subramanya Iyer. The idea of using variations of the word 'Venkatesa' as the mudra can also be said to have been modeled after Tyagaraja who has employed variations like 'Tyagarājanuta', 'Tyagarājavinuta', 'Tyagarajārchita',

'Tyagaraja karārchita', 'Tyagaraja Gireesa Vinuta' etc. Swati Tirunal has adopted an even more flexible step of using all the Sanskrit equivalents of the lotus flower in conjunction with the word 'Nābha', 'Padmanābha', 'Sarasijanābha', 'Kamalanābha', 'Sarojanābha', 'Varijanābha' etc. Patnam Subramanya Iyer has followed Tyagarja in the practice of incorporating the signature only in the concluding portion of the song, more often in the last line itself. Vasudevachar, a disciple of Patnam Subramanya Iyer has, however, chosen to introduce his mudra 'Vasudeva' not necessarily at the end of the song but at any convenient juncture in any part of song, sometimes in the very first line. Example: 'Pāhikrishna Vasudeva' (Behag) in the first line, "Idi Neeku Nyāyama" (Gamanasrama), last word in the last line, "Brochevarevarura" (Khamas) penultimate line, "Bhajare Mānasa" (Abheri) second line. Vasudevachar seems to have taken cue from the great Muthuswamy Dikshitar who has employed his mudra 'Guruguha' in any part of the kriti found appropriate by him, though majority of his kritis bear the mudra towards the end. There are also songs in which the very first word of the song is the mudra. Example: "Guruguhāya" in Sama raga. In "Mānasa Guruguha" (Ananda Bhairavi) and "Sri Guruguha" (Devakriya) the second word is the mudra. His very first song "Srinādādi Guruguho" (Mayamalava Goula) has the mudra in the opening line itself as the third word.

CONVERSATIONAL LYRIC

Among the Trinity, the lyrical appeal of the compositions is more telling in Tyagaraja mainly because he has liberally utilized colloquial and conversational language. Since Dikshitar's medium was Sanskrit which is not a spoken language, his lyric will not easily appeal to a common man. Syāma Sastry did mainly use only Telugu but his range of variety was limited, since he addressed all his kritis only to one Goddess, more often in a rasa evoking pity as in a child's entreaties to the mother. But Tyagaraja's canvas was far wider since he had sung the narration of practically the whole of Ramayan besides songs in praise of other Godheads. As a story teller Tyagaraja's necessity and scope for covering most of the rasas must have been very wide. His devotion to Rama was such that many of his songs are patterned as a conversation between him and the God in various moods. A typical example would be the song in Sankarabharana "Yeduta Nilachite needu sommu yēmi pōdura" Adi tala. Such a catchy conversational opening of a song cannot be expected in an unspoken language like Sanskrit. The above line "Yeduta Nilachite" is virtual prose sentence in an idiomatic language that people use often in day-to-day talks. Instead of formally begging for a Darshan of the God, Tyagaraja uses the common man's language and says "What would you loose (OH Rama) if you condescend to come before me? Would your ancestral properties diminish if you do so?" The English translation of this line is nowhere near to Telugu expression in the instantaneous effect it would produce on a lay listener. Addressing God with such liberty has been the privilege of ardent devotees in all religious communities of our country. Slightly more angry attitude is seen in the wordings of kritis like 'Adigi Sukhamu Yevvaru Pondiri' (Madhyamavati), 'Ilalo Pranatārthi Harudani' (Athana), which are in the Nindāstuti variety.

As in many other aspects, Patnam Subramanya Iyer has religiously followed Tyagaraja in the pattern of lyric in his compositions. There is, however, a noticeable difference between the two. While Telugu was the mother tongue of Tyagaraja, knowledge of that language must have been acquired by study by Patnam Subramanya Iyer whose mother tongue was Tamil. The latter's language would, therefore, sound rather too prosaic at times. An example of this would be 'Intakante Kāvalena I Kashtamu Chālada' (Kannada raga). The language in the whole kriti is in the same vein. 'Chitukante Rōga Peeditamai' and 'Mattikunda Kante Heenamainadi' in 'Yetunamminavo' (Saveri) are also expressions in too open prose order. It is noteworthy that the same Patnam Subramanya Iyer has changed into a lyric which is a mere collection of epithets in his Sanskrit compositions—'Nijadāsa Varada' (Kalyani) and 'Raghuvamsa' (Kadanakuthuhalam). Between Tyagaraja and Patnam Subramanya Iyer there has been a gap of nearly a century during which time human life must have become more materialistic. While it is easily accepted that Tyagaraja who took to sanyāsa ashram only in last few days of his life, would have been saintly right from his child-hood, it is not uncommon to think of Patnam Subramanya Iyer as anything more than a mere orthodox grihasta and never as a Swāmiji. In this backgroud, a difference is sure to exist in the impact of the lyric of the two even when they might have used words relating to the same theme of a dialogue between the devotee and the Lord or anything else philosophical.

***

4

Critical Appreciation of One Varnam, One Kriti and One Javali of Patnam Subramanya Iyer

A critical analysis of Patnam Subramanya Iyer's Varnam-"Valachi Vachchi": Varnams occupy a very important place in the realm of music compositions. They are technical pieces of serious classical music with purposes more than one for various levels of learners and listeners. Composer of a varnam must be equipped with musical acumen and creative ability of a very high order, in certain respects even more than the caliber needed for composing kritis. A more explicit rhythm, comparatively a more catchy music and more of lyrical appeal are the aspects in which a kriti could mainly differ from a Varnam, the main purpose of which is to remain as sort of thesaurus for the grammar of the Raga. Only a person with a sure grip with the classical idiom of a raga can compose a varnam which aims to portray the raga not only through the medium of the lyric but also in mere swaras. Methodical practising of varnams gives a hold for a learner to progress and delve deeper into the ocean of classicism. Even an experienced musician will have occasions to check up with a varnam when in doubt about the appropriateness of a given phrase in a particular raga. He can also improve his command over the raga be keenly looking into the passages shown in a varnam.

NAVARAGAMALIKA VARNAM — ADI TALAM

1. Kedaram

Pallavi: Valachi Vachchi Yunna Nāpai
Chalamu Sēya Mera Gādura

2. Sankarabharanam

Anupallavi: Cheluvudaina Sri Venkatesa
Kalasimelasi Kaugalinchara

3. Yadukulakambhoji

Charanam: Padasarojamula Ne Nammiti

A composer of a varnam should thus have has a lot more to say about a particular raga than a mere practitioner. The former's rapport with that raga must be so intense that he is able to contain and enshrine so much of the inexhaustive facets of the raga in a few āvartās of the varnam with the constraints of the Tala, Lyric and Swarams. Composing a Ragamalika varnam is all the more a challenge to the composer.

In 'valachivachchi', Patnam Subramanya Iyer has conformed to the usual practice of those days by employed lyric with the Sringara Rasa. Any person with a good knowledge in Telugu would be able to notice that the vocabulary employed in varnams of all composers in generation is of a limited range and the repetition of common place words like 'Vanajākshi', 'Ninnukori', Viribōni', 'Mārubari', 'Sāmininne' etc. Uniform adherence to this habit of using hackneyed clichés by all composers has even given rise to sort of a convention that varnams should always be composed with oft-used and familiar words like those mentioned above. It can be said of Patnam Subramanya Iyer that he has been taking more pains in choosing appropriate Telugu words for his compositions and he is generally free from blatant grammatical mistakes. But even he has treaded the beaten-track in this Navaragamalika Varnam by including the usual phrases like 'Chalamuseyaka', 'Cheluvudaina', and 'Padasarojamula Nammiti'. Lyrics in sringara vein are all right for javalis and padams but it is surprising why even varnams of those days employed only the same type of sahityam. It might be the influence of pada varna which were meant for Abhinaya in dance concerts.

Sahityam apart, the music (Dhātu) of the varnam 'Valachivachchi' measures up very well to the purposes intended in varnam. The raga bhava of the various ragas has been prominently brought out. Patnam Subramanya Iyer seems to have deliberately chosen closely related ragas like Kedaram, Sankarabharanam, Kalyani and Begada in succession apart from Kambhoji and Yadukula Kambhoji and Bilahari. This is perhaps to explain to the learners how the time honoured ragas are able to maintain their identity even when two of these ragas of approximating swara structure are sung one immediately after the other. Patnam Subramanya Iyer has done an admirable job in this rope-walking though his success with Kambhoji and Yadukula Kambhoji cannot be said to be cent-percent. The conventional rule of prosody like Dviteeyākshara Prāsa has been observed between the pallavi (Valachi) and the anupallavi (Cheluvu). There is telling swarakshara in the charana 'Padasaroja', Srotovahayati has been employed in the Bilahari Yettugada swaram.

g p d Ṡ

r g p d Ṡ

s r g p d Ṡ

ḍ s r g P

This varnam thus has sample evidence to the overall command Patnam Subramanya Iyer had with the classical idiom of ragas, and rhythm and the art of composing varnams.

A CRITICAL ANALYSIS OF THE KRITI 'MANASUNA NERA NAMMITI' IN BEGADA

Patnam Subramanya Iyer is said to have been called "Begada Subramanya Iyer" and indication of his penchant for this raga is given by the fact that he has composed two songs in this and has included it in the Navarāgamalika Varnam also. The two kritis portray the raga from different angles and give a lot of lead for learners and musicians to sing alapana and swarm. 'Abhimāna' starts with the phrase s ṇ ḍ p in stately mandra sthāyi while 'Manasuna' starts with the another characteristic phrase of the raga m g m p d p ṡ and explores the Madhya and tara sthāyis. The former kriti is rhythmically more catchy and still brings out a lot of raga bhava. The tightness of rhythm is explicit because of the Eduppu in the half of little finger. This Eduppu has been widely employed only by Tyagaraja and his scions. Patnam Subramanya Iyer seems to have liked this Eduppu and has employed it in many of his compositions. The other Begada kriti "Manasuna" seeks to reveal in raga bhava, keeping the rhythm is tight under-current.

LYRIC

Telugu has somehow been the most preferred medium for compositions in classical music. The reasons for this are many and an analysis of this needs to be dealt with separately. We will limit ourselves here to the statement of the fact that there have been many composers belonging to various mother tongues composing their kritis only in Telugu, often not composing even a single composition in their mother tongue. Patnam Subramanya Iyer, Mysore Vasudevachar, and Poochchi Srinivasa Iyengar are prominent among such composers. It should be worthwhile mentioning here that there is not even a single case of a composer whose mother tongue is Telugu composing entirely in other language. The overwhelming influence of Tyagaraja, the king among the composers is one major factor in making all other composers fall in line and keep Telugu as the lingua-franca. In all the Telugu compositions of non-Andhra composers it is easily seen that they have conceived their ideas only in their mother tongue and then converted the same into Telugu expressions made of the limited vocabulary that they might have acquired. Many such composers had a narrow range of vocabulary in Telugu and it shows in their compositions. Among such composers Patnam Subramanya Iyer and Vasudevachar occupy a very high rank in command over Telugu. The Telugu found in the songs of these two composers is almost entirely free from grammatical inaccuracies. One would still feel the difference between the Telugu of Kshetragna and that of Patnam Subramanya Iyer. It is obviously because Kshetragna was an Andhra by birth and breed and he could straight away think in his mother tongue and sing in it with abandon while the non-Telugu composers have to rely upon their acquired knowledge of the languages and could not burst into poetry of that language. Even those hailing originally form Andhra Pradesh but domiciled in Tamil Nadu are very likely to have lost the natural grip of the Telugu language because of the necessity of their having to deal only in Tamil in day-to-day life. In the Telugu of such composers there are chances of occurrences of Telugu words that may be outlandish to a native Andhra. Some Andhras find inadequacies even in the compositions of Tyagaraja whose mother tongue was, of course, Telugu but he lived all his life in the heart of Tamil Nadu. Tyagaraja and many others like him fused Sanskrit liberally in Telugu songs. Patnam Subramanya Iyer did not draw from Sanskrit so liberally as Tyagaraja and he has even attempted colloquial and conversational Telugu. It is still possible to find out from his kritis that the flow of language is not that of a native Andhra.

The sahitya of 'Manasuna Nera Nammiti' follows the Sūtra-Vritti-Bhāshya formula of Tyagaraja who usually makes a suggestive statement in the pallavi, expands it in the anupallavi and explains and annotates the same in the charanam. In this pattern the sāhityam of 'Manasuna' runs as follows:

Pallavi	:	Manasuna Nera Nammiti Nee Mahimalu Vini Nē Satatamu
Anupallavi	:	Anagha Nannetlaina Adarinchi Brotuvanuchu
Charanam	:	Krurudaina Kākāsurudu Kori Saranamanaga Natani Krura Krutyamulaku Neeve Kopimpaka Kāchinatula Neramento Nē Jēsinanu Neeve Mannintu Vanuchu Vāranārti Harana Sri Varada Venkateswara Ninnu

The Pallavi states that the Bhakta has confidence, the Anupallavi says what the confidence is, and the Charana explains how the confidence came. The Pallavi and Anupallavi extol the Lord's unlimited mercy and compassion towards people and the Charana narrates the Kākāsura episode of Ramayana wherein the Lord is famed as a saviour of even a demon who had actually wronged mother Seeta herself. If even such a wrong-doer can be pardoned and saved why not me, another lesser mortal?, the composer asks. The words used in the kriti are common place, some of them even hackneyed (Nammiti, Ādarinchi, Brotuvanuchu etc.). The word 'Krūra' occurs twice and this could have been avoided. The word 'Neeve' also comes twice. The first two pādās of the Charanam seem to be rather verbose. The idea can as well as be conveyed in less number of words. The third pādā 'Nēramento' reminds us of the comparable portion 'Neerajākshikai' in the Devagāndhari song 'Ksheera Sāgara' of Tyāgaraja. In the latter the pādā 'Neerajākshi' is Dhātu-wise not essential and the kriti would be musically complete and wholesome even without this portion, though Mātu-wise it serves some purpose. In Patnam Subramanya Iyer 'Manasuna' – the portion 'Nēramento... Vanuchu' does not contribute much to Begada and even lyric-wise it is easy to delete this portion and still convey the message of the whole song. The last pādā which has Dhātu like the Anupallavi is true to the tradition established by Tyagaraja. Irrespective of all this critical discussion about the sāhitya of the song it should be an indisputed fact that this song is a gem in the raga Begada, justifying the title Begada Subramanya Iyer to the composer.

A CRITICAL APPECIATION OF A JAVALI OF PATNAM SUBRAMANYA IYER

Javalis are all in rakti ragas, which along with their characteristic tempo, bring out well their amorous theme, akin to the PADAS. These dazzling little pieces are now quite familiar to us who have heard them in the closing part of the concert-programmes but they are of recent, origin.

The Javali like 'Kavadichindu' shows how, till recent times, the creative power of our music was active in putting forth new and delightful forms.

Curiously for a type which has come up in times so near to us, the Javali is really obscure in its origins. It's very name is intriguing. Kittu's Kannada Dictionary notes Javali as a kind of lewd poetry. Maharashtra scholars assure us that it is not a Marathi word. The Tamil Lexicon (p. 3874) mentions JAVALI as derived from Urdu JHWALI, but no authority is cited there and Persian and Urdu scholars are not able to confirm this. The word does not occur among the numerous Desi musical terms found in music works. While the possibility of connecting it with some Sanskrit words (Example: Capala, Kannada Javala) is there, it must be confessed that the name is mysterious. In Telugu, only later Dictionaries of the last quarter of the last century note the word and in the Telugu region too Javali composers had come up only in the later part of the last century. In fact, the JAVALI as a composition came into being and prominence only in the later part of the last century.

Javalis are meant to create an instant appeal with listeners of all levels. While on this effort a margin is given to Javali in the matter of strict adherence to the grammer of the Raga. This liberty even exceeds limit in some Javalis. Example: Charanam of 'Apadūruku' Khamas and the Charanam of 'Sarasamulādetanduku' Kapi. There is also one popular Javali 'Sāmirādāyane' which does not conform to any single raga and is more like a folk tune. There are also other hybrid Javalis in Manipravalam with mixture of English words too. (0 my lovely lalana-Kharaharapriya). Patnam Subramanya Iyer is also said to have composed on the frivuolus theme like his own addiction to the snuff powder.

The instant musical appeal of the javalis have made them popular not only in Music and Dance concerts but also in Dramas and Cinemas. The following is an indicative list of javalis and corresponding songs which were popular on the stage or celluloid word too:

1. 'Yela Rādāyene'-Bhairavi
   Adopted in 'Unaikkandu' sung by the hero M.K. Tyagaraja Bhagavatar in the film 'Gunālan'.
2. 'Cheli Nēnetlu'-in Pharaz
   Adopted in 'Maravene' sung by M.S. Subbalakshmi in the film 'Meera'.
3. 'Yemandunemo Muddu Balamani'-in Kapi corresponds to 'Kandipan Maithuna' sung by S.G. Kittappa, the immortal hero of the dramas.

There is a permissible lightness in not only the tune but also in the lyric that augments the instant appeal of the Javalis. The theme is always about the love and infatuation between humans entangled in a love triangle. More often Javalis vent the feelings of an aggrieved lady who pours out her anguish at the misdemeanour of the lover. Such a theme in a Javali or any song is sure to instantly appeal to a common listener and the music of the Javali is also of a matching catchyness.

RAGAM: SURATI — RUPAKA TALAM

Pallavi : Mariyāda Teliyakane
Mātaladuta Tagunate

Anupallavi : Parihāsamu Jēya Tagina
Varusa Kaligiyunte Nēmi

Charanam : 1. Sarasa Sallapamulaku
Samayamu Kādāde Yeme

Sarasijākshi Nāvanti
Satulu Gumpugūdi Yundaga
2. Veladiro Nannu Gūdinatlu
Venkateswarudu Neepai
Balavantamuga Nanu
Valachi Vachchina Nēmi

Patnam Subramanya Iyer's Javalis bear evidence to the composer's detailed knowledge about this genre among compositions. His Javali in the raga 'Surati' is a classic example. While all his kritis are generally about God and the Devotees appeal to Him in various moods, the theme of this Javali is the expression of a lady's disapproval and express of concern about the unbecoming behaviour of the hero. Like the sahitya the music is also falling sweet and light on the ears. The surati raga employed in Kshetragna Pada 'Kontigādu' and the Padavarnam 'Sāmi Yentani' by Subbarama Dikshitar are touchstone for the classical excellence and weight of the raga. In Tyagaraja's 'Geetharthamu' the weight can be said to have eased a little and a further step in that direction is what we have seen in 'Mariyāda Teliyakane' the javali of appropriate Dhātu and Mātu. In spite of the liberities taken the Javali still remains within limits and can very well be classified among compositions in the classical fold. The Javali has a flashy opening, unfolding the classic appeal of Surati. Ragas like Behag or Khamas or Kapi have the advantage of a built-in Sringara Rasa in the very nature of the raga. But surati is not so patently structured in a Sringara vein and a composer of a Javali in the raga should take pains to explore the particular contours of the raga that would fit a Javali. Patnam Subramanya Iyer has done this admirably well. Giving accent to Madhyamam in Surati, for instance, would sound rather heavy (Geethārthamu starts with

Madhyamam) and Patnam Subramanya Iyer has judiciously avoided this in the Javali. The tessiture of this javali is aptly within an octave and half, that too mainly around Tāra Shadja. Permissible liberty with the grammar of the raga has also been taken in one of the sangatis in the pallavi in the phrase

p d d n ṡ n d p m M g
Ma.......ri.............ya

This prayoga has since come to stay as a visesha sanchara for Surati. This occurs, of course in Kshetragna's 'Kontigādu' and also in Subbarama Dikshitar's Padavarnam. The music of this javali is pleasing to the listeners and inspiring to the singer while providing a model for seekers of beauty in raga alapana. In short this javali will easily vouch the exalted place occupied by Patnam Subramanya Iyer among composers of classical music.

The lyric of this composition also conforms to the norms of javali. It freely uses colloquial expressions like 'Mātalādatagunate', Tagina Varusa Kaligiyunte', 'Sarasa Sallāpamulaku Samayamu Kāde', etc. Addressing fellow women as 'Yeme' is indeed too earthy a language. The sahitya of this javali is indded very authentic and appreciable, all the more as especially it is from a composer whose mother tongue is not Telugu.

❊ ❊ ❊

5

Patnam Subramanya Iyer's Contemporaries

More prominent among the contemporaries of Patnam Subramanya Iyer were:

1. Krishna Swamy Ayyah	(1839-1917)
2. Neela Kanta Sivan	(1839-1900)
3. Subbarama Dikshitar	(1839-1904)
4. Pallavi Sesha Iyer	(1842-1909)
5. Maha Vaidyanatha Iyer	(1844-1893)
6. Rama Swamy Siwan	(1839-1897)
7. Tiruvattiyur Tyagayyar	(1845-1917)
8. Achuta Dasa	(1850-1902)
9. Veena Seshanna	(1852-1926)
10. Karur Chinna Devudu Iyer	(1861-1901)
11. Tachur Singaracharyulu Brothers	(1834-1892)
12. Annaswami Sastry	(1827-1900)
13. Mysore Sadasiva Rao	(1826-1906)

Among these Maha Vaidyanatha Sivan must be studied concurrently because he and Patnam Subramanya Iyer lived in the same town in nearly streets for major part of their lives. Though they had mutual regard, their admirers formed rival groups and created an atmosphere of enimity between the two illustrious musicians. It is appropriate here to study the life sketch of the former also.

After the Carnatic music Tritnity-Tyagaraja, Muthuswamy Dikshitar and Syama Sastry-no name has endeared itself to people in the South as much as that of Maha Vaidyanatha Iyer. In his biography of this celebrated musician, the great Tamil scholar and savant Mahamahopadhyaya Dr. U.V. Swaminatha Iyer (who was not given to exaggeration) says: "Very rarely does the music world come across a musician of the caliber of Maha Vaidyanatha Iyer. He was unique in many ways and one in a thousand in the field of music. His divine personality infused music with a new spirit. Tamil Nadu was blessed to have had him".

(Maha) Vaidyanatha Iyer (also known as Sivan) was born in 1844, some three years before Tyagaraja passed away. He was the third son of Panchanada Iyer alias Duraiswami Iyer, of Vaiyacheri in Tanjore district, a village noted for its rich religious and cultural traditions. His elder brother was Ramaswami Sivan, from whom he was inseparable throughout his life. His mother came to the line of the famous composers, Anai and Aiya of the Tanjore royal court. Duraiswami Iyer too belonged to a family of musicians.

Even from childhood the two brothers, Ramaswami and Vaidyanathan displayed remarkable aptitude for music, and they were both trained by their father. Vaidyanatha Iyer, in particular, was endowed with a divine voice possessing charm, grace, range and fast delivery. The elder brother had a special taste for Tamil literature and he specialized in it in addition to music. After some time the father put them both under the tutelage of Manambuchavadi Venkatasubbayyar, pupil of Tyagaraja and renowned musician, scholar and composer.

The boys learnt higher Lakshya and Lakshana from the great master.

At the very early age of seven, Vaidyanatha Iyer attained proficiency in Ragam-Tanam-Pallavi, the high water-mark of creative art in Carnatic Music. His gifted voice had a range of over three octaves and he could manipulate six degrees of speed. It was not long before the prodigy's talent was recognized and patronized. He was invited for concerts in connection with marriages and other festivities. In concerts his brother Ramaswami Iyer sat by his side playing the Tambura and singing in accompaniment to him.

At the age of ten, within three years of his entering the profession, Vaidyanatha Iyer was invited to the Pudukottai Darbar which was adorned by eminent musicians like Veena Subbukkutti Iyer. His great merit was duly recognized there and, shortly thereafter, he was invited to the Darbar's of Ramanathapuram and Ettayapuram, not to speak of the many other patrons of the southern districts.

The Tiruvaduturai religious mutt has a long tradition of patronage to music and literature. At the time Vaidyanatha Iyer came into prominence Sri Subramanya Desikar, perhaps the greatest and most enlightened patron in the history of the mutt, was the junior pontiff at Kallidaikurichi in Tirunelveli district. He invited Vaidyanatha Iyer and made him sing among, and in a contest with, the famous musicians, Peria (senior) Vaidyanatha Iyer and Chinna (junior) Vaidyanatha Iyer, whom he was just a boy of 12, but he surpassed the veterans. He elaborated the raga Chakravākam for the first time in history. In recognition of his mastery young Vaidyanatha Iyer was awarded the title

'Maha' (great) prefixed to his name. Thenceforth he was known as Maha Vaidyanatha Iyer.

The great musician's fame spread far and wide, and he was invited thrice to the Travancore Darbar where he won the appreciation of such musicians of eminence as Parameswara Bhagavatar and Coimbatore Raghava Iyer. He was also invited thrice to the Mysore Darbar. The Raja of Venkatagiri, who was a scholar in music, honoured him with double Sanmanam just for the pleasure and benefit of a musicological discussion with him.

His brother Ramaswami Sivan composed many songs and more particularly, a big devotional work called "Periya Purāna Kirtanaigal". Vaidyanatha Iyer himself composed, under the signature "Guhadasa", classical compositions and verses in Sanskrit and Tamil. Besides, he gave the music and a new text for the 75-mela Ragamalika which was in archives of the Tanjore palace. A study of the ragamalika would reveal how he contrived to avoid undue dissonance and extract the semblance of Raga from Vivādi Melās. For the rest, his voice was there.

Maha Vaidyanatha Iyer's popularity was not confined to the elite. His magical voice, inspired music, and sense of proportion and propriety-all these stood him in good stead with the general public also. They thronged to hear him. The duration of his concert was from 1½ to 2 hours only, with the major part devoted to Ragam-Tanam-Pallavi and the rest to two or three compositions and short ālāpanās. It was pure music par excellence. For applied music in the form of devotional songs and verses, for which too he was greatly in demand, he usually gave a second performance on the following day. His musical discourses (Sivākathās) progagated Bhakti (piety) along with Rakti (aesthetic delight). He was a legend in his own time.

He was deeply religious, simple and unassuming but not wanting in wit or worldly wisdom. His radiant personality exuded charm, grace and humility, and a confidence born of disciplined living. Independent as he was, he did not, as Tyagaraja had done before him, shun patronage, princely or popular. Patronage in those days meant homage. He wa rewarded handsomely for his concerts but payment was not considered "the price". It was Sanmānam, the respect shown to the learned. Nor was there any stipulation. The story is told of how, a few years before his death, when for a concert of his at Madras the organizers collected "gate money". Maha Vaidyanatha Iyer, coming to know of it, indignantly refused to sing where they "sold" music. Evidently those were the twilight years of musical independence and enlightened patronage.

During his career he changed his residence from Vaidyacheri to Tiruvaiyaru. A number of pupils and admirers stayed in his house and were fed by him. He did not, however, teach anyone directly. His singing was sufficient inspiration to them. Lessons were given to some by his brother Ramaswami Sivan. Among his well-known pupils were Ramanathapuram Poochchi Srinivasa Iyengar and Umayalpuram Swaminatha Iyer.

Maha Vaidyanatha Iyer gave new dimensions of creative interpretation to some of the compositions of the Trinity, and tradition (as distinguished form orthodoxy) accepted them. It was he who gave a new tempo and popularity to Dikshitar's 'Vatapiganapatim' in the raga Hamsadhvani. Great as his gifts were even from childhood, he did not, we learn, let go any opportunity to improve his musicianship, scholarship and literary attainments. When he died in 1893, at the early age of 49, the world of Carnatic Music felt that it had lost the greatest musician since Tyagaraja.

The voices and styles of Patnam Subramanya Iyer and Maha Vaidyanatha Sivan had individual merits of dissimilar nature. While Maha Vaidyanatha Sivan had a comparatively thin and fast moving voice, Patnam Subramanya Iyer was known for a heavy voice with a rugged charm. While the former's forte was Dhurita Kāla, the latter specialized in stately Chowka and Madhyama Kālas. Both were famous both as composers and performers. Maha Vaidyanatha Sivan would seem to have had a tendency for virtuosity. He has taken pains to structure the marathan ragamalika employing the entire 72 melakarta with raga mudra too. In all his compositional efforts his brother Ramaswamy Sivan collaborated. Patnam Subramanya Iyer had no penchant for such feats but he concentrated on the rakti element and composed kritis, varnams and javali's that would be of immediate utility in concerts. He had no fancy for Raga Mudra, Ragamalika, Vivadi Melas etc. He seems to have attempted to further consolidate some of the new ragas brought into vogue by Tyagaraja. Example: Malavi, Narayani, Mandari. He has in fact composed two songs in Mandari "Ninnu Jeppa Kāranamemi" Adi tala, 'Yendukitu Chapalamu' Misra chapu and still one is not sure whether the status of Mandari has really enhanced from where it was in Tyagaraja's 'Paralokabhaya', Adi tala. In the other two ragas Malavi, and Narayani, however, Patnam Subramanya Iyer has succeeded by exhibiting mere insights.

Another notable contemporary to Patnam Subramanya

Iyer was Tiruvottiyur Tyagayyar, son of Veena Kuppayyar. Tiruvottiyur is today a suburb of the city of Madras. During Patnam Subramanya Iyer's time Tiruvottiyur might have been a village in proximity to the city of Madras. Patnam Subramanya Iyer was perhaps the first famous musician to have lived in a cosmopolitan city like Madras. Most other musicians of those days live in or around their native villages or the neighbouring towns. Offering prayers at the village temples, bathing in the sacred river or tank and observing all the religious rituals was a way of life to everybody in those days including musicians. The approach to the art of music was one of surrender, reverence and awe as opposed to the deplorably commercial attitude that is rampant today. Almost all famous musicians of the current times have migrated to Madras city in search of livelihood through music, oblivious of what sort of use the great art of music is put to. Music might not have been so widely known as it is today, but to the small number of musicians and patrons of those days it was certainly a highly respected art of divinity and city life was not considered essential for artists. The very fact that the prefix 'Patnam' was annexed to Subramaya Iyer's name shows how he was the rare and first specimen of a classical musician opting to migrate to the city. The history of Madras turning into a Mecca of music that it is today must have origined from the days when Patnam Subramanya Iyer started living at Madras (he shifted back to Tiruvaiyaru towards end of his life) with his contemporary Tyagayyar living in Tiruvottiyur, quite close by. Tyagayyar was also a composer more known through his varnams. He does not seem to have been a popular performing artist like Patnam Subramanya Iyer and it is not known whether the two composers were in frequent touch. But we can infer that composing varnams must have become a popular pursuit at their time. Some other contemporaries like Subbarama Dikshitar, Pallavi Seshayyar, Veena Seshanna, Karur Brothers, Tachur Singaracharyulu Brothers, Annaswamy Sastry and Mysore Sadasiva Rao have all been noted composers. This shows that attempt at creating own compositions by musicians of those days was not considered sacrilegious as it is done today, at least in some quarters.

Subbarama Dikshitar is another illustrious contemporary of Patnam Subramanya Iyer. Though not much of a performing artist Subbarama Dikshitar was kept in very high esteem by the people and fellow musicians. He is perhaps the most prominent vidvan whose magnum-opus, the Sangeeta Sampradaya Pradarshini is one book that continues to enjoy earnest following even by practical musicians who are generally known for their dis-inclination for any written material on music. The Sangeeta Sampradaya Pradarshini has some very rare virtues. It was easily the first gigantic work of that magnitude to bring out a large number of traditional kritis in scientific notation. In an earnest effort to effectively convey the sophisticated music of Dikshitar in the medium of written material Subbarama Dikshitar invented many signs and symbols. This was indeed a monumental task, especially in those days when the art of printing had just begun to gain vogue in South India. The Sangeeta Sampradaya Pradarshini is thus of valuable material to researchers in many subjects. Any research on Dikshitar kritis can not proceed without consulting this book. For those who want to write a dissertation on the topic of Musical Notation this book is of inevitable importance. Apart from this Subbarama Dikshitar has also covered vast areas of applied musicology in this book and in addition has also given the biographies of all luminaries in the field of music, right from the days of Bharata to his own period. He has even given his own biography with a mention of his musically talented son too. This book is, therefore, a veritable bible for musicians, musicologists, students, teachers and lovers of music in general. Among his contemporaries Subbarama Dikshitar has mentioned Patnam Subramanya Iyer also as a musician and composer of eminence. He has, however, not chosen to include compositions of Patnam Subramanya Iyer in the main body of the book which has been devoted for major part to compositions of Muthuswamy Dikshitar with a minor portion allotted to other composers including his own self. The period of Patnam Subramanya Iyer, Subbarama Dikshitar and their illustrious contemporaries listed in the beginning of this chapter seems to have been a prosperous time for classical music. Renowned musicians, Lakshana Lakshya Vidwans, authors, composers, teachers and above all enlightened patrons—all these tribes have flourished in this significant epoch.

Even today there are many composers but the popularity of post-Trinity composers can never be lost. This is because of the knowledge of music and deep insight into ragabhava that the latter possessed. Our contemporary composers may not be musicians themselves thus creating a situation where composers outnumber musicians. It took more than half a century for the Trinity's compositions to appear in print and they have survived sheerly by merit and through aural traditions. In these days publishing one's work has become a very common practice and even before a particular composition is sung or listened to, with respect.

In the midst of such composers who are influential or rich or both, the survival of a composer of genuine merit who lacks the facility for self promotion, is very difficult. His or her talent may go un-noticed and may not contribute to the growth of the art while the music field may be flooded with compositions. For this art to be recognised and respected by our future generations, we must realise that it is quality of music and not its quantity which matters. If we wish to be heard and regarded in the same way as Trinity or post-Trinity composers, we must deeply analyse their compositions and produce compositions comparable to their merit.

❋❋❋

6

Patnam Subramanya Iyer's Disciples

POOCHCHI SRINIVASA IYENGAR

Even as Patnam Subramanya Iyer was a faithful treader of Tyagaraja's musical path, Poochchi Srinivasa Iyengar the famous disciple of the former carried the tradition to the succeeding generations. He made a mark both as a performing musician and as a composer. Like his guru he too has given us kritis, varnams, javalis and tillanas some in each of which have deservedly become popular in concert music. His 'Saraguna Pālimpa' a gem in the ragam kedaragaula is alone enough to prove the grip he had with the classical idiom. In the art of appending chittasvarams he can even be said to have excelled Patnam Subramanya Iyer. His penchant for chittaswaram was such that he did not spare even a javali. His 'Veganeevu' (Surati) has a chittaswaram but it is not being sung by many artists. It is said that he learnt from both Patnam Subramanya Iyer and Maha Vaidyanatha Sivan who were arch rivals and it is surprising that he could emerge as a famous person himself without getting disintegrated in the heat that existed between the two gurus. It is not exactly known how the prefix "Poochchi" got to be attached to his name. One version is that he had a brisk voice and his style was matchingly mobile and virulent, tempting the listeners to liken his music to the ceaseless brisk flying of some insects which are called in Tamil as "Poochi". Like his guru he too chose to compose only in Telugu and Sanskrit, leaving his mother tongue (Tamil) aside. But his inadequate command over Telugu betrays often and in quite a few places the sahitya portion of his songs is not acceptable to the Andhras.

Examples:

1. Charanam of 'Saraguna Palimpa' where he was used the phrase 'Gaja Rajudu' assuming that to be same in declention as 'Ramudu' or 'Krishnudu'.
2. Charanam of 'Samajavarada'—Suddasaveri.
   Though there were many other minor composers and musicians in his period Poochchi Srinivasa Iyengar did achieve a separate status and has earned a place in the list of luminaries in the post-Trinity era.

MYSORE VASUDEVACHAR

Another meritorious composer whose impact has belatedly surfaced in recent times is Mysore Vasudevachar. Though the Karnataka area was the place in which Purandara Dasa and others of the Dasakuta lived and preached and though the awareness and taste for classical music is quite wide and large in that area. One of the Mysore Maharajas himself was a composer and some of his compositions are of good merit. Ex. 'Sri Maha Ganapatim' (Atana), 'Ksheera Sagara' (Mayamalava Goula) but his compositions are yet to arrive in full. Another noted name is that of Mysore Sadasiva Rao who did not actually belong to Mysore but hailed from Tamil Nadu. 'Saketa Nagara' (Harikambhoji) was a kriti of his that was very famous at one time. His kritis in the rare raga Balahamsa are also known in informed circles. Though the merit in his compositions cannot be denied his compositions have not left a lasting impact. That leaves us with only one name, Mysore Vasudevachar, who is perhaps the most well known composer from Karnataka area since Purandara Dasa, Vasudevachar's "Brochevarevarura" (Khamas), "Rara Rajeeva Lochana" (Mohana) became very popular in many parts of the country even during his life time. In the recent tendency to highlight composers, Vasudevachar's name has also had a boost, a deserved one at that. Like most others he too composed only in Sanskrit and Telugu leaving his mother tongue Kannada aside. Compared to Poochchi Srinivasa Iyengar and many others, the Telugu of Mysore Vasudevachar is almost flawless and natural and his Sanskrit too is mellifluous. He can be said to have been more versatile and innovative than many of his contemporaries. He is equally at home in both single and two kalai kritis and has successfully experimented kritis in rare talas like Khanda Triputa, Misra Triputa and Tisra Triputa. Examples: Dasarathe-Bilahari-Tisra Triputa, 'Mama Hridaye'-Ritigoula-Khanda Triputa and 'Pranatārthi Harnana'-Senjurutti-Khanda Triputa, 'Pranamamyaham'-Ranjani-Misra Triputa. Another achievement is the classical weight he has infused in kritis in light ragas like Maund, Behag, Abheri etc. Some of his chittasvarams are of such overwhelming appeal as to outshine and eclipse the very kritis to which they are appended.

Example:

> 'Pranatarthihara' (Senjurutti) 'Brochevarevarura' (Khamas) 'Rara Rajeeva Lochana' (Mohanam). There are group kritis also to his credit like the Vishnu nama kritis, Lakshmi and Saraswathy Pancharatnams. Mysore Vasudevachar's contribution to the music field has thus been significant and long lasting.

❋ ❋ ❋

7

Adi Tala Varnams of Patnam Subramanya Iyer

(Lyrics with Notation)

ADI TALA VARNAMS (TANA VARNAMS)

1. PALUMĀRU

Ragam : NATTAI – 36th Chalanāta Janyam

Talam : ADI

Arohanam : S R_3 G_3 M_1 P D_3 N_3 Ṡ

Avarohanam : Ṡ N_3 P M_1 R_3 S

Pallavi : Palumāru Ninne Kōriyunna
Nāpai pantamela Jesevurā ‖

Anupallavi : Ilalo Velayu Sri Seshachala Nivāsa Śri
Venkatesā

Charanam : Saarvabhauma Nannelukora

1. पलुमारू

राग : नाट

तालम् : आदि

पल्लवि

पलुमारू निन्ने कोरियुन्न नापै।
पंतमेल जेसेवुरा।।

अनुपल्लवि

इललो वेलयु श्री शेषाचल
निवास श्री वेंकटेश।।

चरणं

सार्वभौमा नन्नेलुकोरा।।

Pallavi 8×4 = 32

P , M , R , , , S Ṇ S R S S Ṇ Ṗ ।
Pa – lu – ma – – – ru – – – Nin – – –

D Ṇ S R G M S M । M R S Ṇ S R G M ॥
ne – – – Ko – ri – yu – nna – Nā – – pai

P M G M R G M R S M G M P , D N ।
Pan – – – ta – – – me – – – la – – –

Ṡ , , Ṡ N P P , । , M R S S R G M ॥
je – – se – – – – vu – – – ra – – –

Anupallavi

N P P N P P M G M P M R G M R S ।
I – – – la – – – lo – – – ve – – –

M G M – P N P– ṠN । P , G M P D N Ṡ ॥
la – – – yu – – Śri – – Śe – śha – – –

N Ṡ Ṙ Ġ Ṁ , Ṙ Ṡ – Ṡ Ṙ Ṡ Ṡ N P D N ।
cha – la – Ni – – – Vā – – – – – sa –

Ṡ Ṙ Ṡ Ṡ   N P P , | M R S– Ṇ   S R G M ||
Śri – – –   Ven – – –   Ka – – te   śa – – –

Mukthāyi Swaram

P M R S – N P M R   S– M R S–   – S, R S |

N Ṡ P ,–   P M R R | G M R S–   M G M P ||

N Ṡ Ṙ N   Ṡ– N Ṡ Ṙ Ġ Ṁ , Ṙ Ṡ   N – P D |

N Ṡ , N   P M– N P, | , M R S   , R G M ||

(Palu)

Charanam

Ṡ , , ,   Ṡ Ṙ Ṡ Ṡ   N P– M   R   R G M R |
Saar – – –   va – – –   – – bhau –   – – – –

S   Ṇ S– Ḍ   Ṇ S– R G | M P M–   G   M P D N ||
ma – – nan   – – ne –   lu – –   ko   – – – ra

Chittai Swaras

1. S , N ,   , P , ,   , M , R   , , S , |
   R , , Ṇ   , , S , | , ,– R G   M P D N ||

(Sarva)

2. Ṡ N P M   ,– G M P   N– P , M   R S Ṇ P̣ |
   Ḍ Ṇ S R   , Ṇ S R | G M ,– P   M P D N ||

(Sarva)

3. Ṡ N P P   M– G M P–   N P M– R   G M R S |
   M G M– P   D N– Ṡ Ṙ | Ġ Ṁ Ṙ Ṡ–   N P D N ||

(Sarva)

4. S P ,– M P N P M– G M P M̤– R S N̤ P̤ |
R S ,– N̤ S R G M | P D N Ṡ N– P D N ||
Ṡ Ṙ Ġ Ṁ , Ṙ S N– Ṙ Ṡ , N– P D N Ṡ |
Ṙ N ,– Ṡ P ,– N M , P M–G M P D N ||

(Sarva)

2. ENDUKINTA MODI

Ragam : SRI — 22nd Kharaharapriya Janyam
Talam : ADI
Arohaṇam : S R_2 M_1 P N_2 Ṡ
Avarohaṇam : Ṡ N_2 P D_2 N_2 P M_1 R_2 G_2 R_2 S
Pallavi : Endukinta Moḍi Jesevura
Ēmi Nēramura Naapai ivela
Anupallavi : Antarangudaina Śri Sundareśwara
nannelukora
Charanam : Nee Saati Evvarunnaru Idharalona

2. एन्दुकिन्त मोडि

राग : श्री
तालम् : आदि

पल्लवि

एन्दुकिन्त मोडि जेसेवुरा
ऐमिनेरमुरा नापै ई वेल।।

अनुपल्लवि

अंतरंगुडैन श्री सुन्दरेश्वर
नन्नेलुकोरा।।

चरणं

नी साटेव्वरुन्नारु ई धरलोन।।

Pallavi 8×4 = 32

R , G ,–	G R S ,–	S R S S–	Ṇ P̣ Ṃ P̣ ।
En – – –	du – – –	Kin – – –	ta – – –
Ṇ S R G	, R–M P ।	M R ,– G	R S Ṇ S ॥
Mo – – ḍi	– – je –	se – – vu	– – ra –
R M P N	, P M–R	G R ,– M	P N–Ṡ Ṙ ।
Ē – mi –	nē – – ra	– – – mu	– – – –
Ṡ , N–P	D N P , ।	M R , G	R S Ṇ S ॥
ra – – nā	– – pai –	I – – ve	– la – –

Anupallavi

P , , N	P M–M ,	, P M R–	R G R S ।
An – – ta	– – ran –	– gu – –	– – – –
N N , P	M–R G R ।	S Ṇ , S	R M P N ॥
ḍai – – –	– – – –	na – – –	Śri – – –
Ṡ , N P–	Ṙ , Ṙ– Ġ	Ṙ Ṡ N ,	P– P N N ।
Sun – – –	da – – re	– śwa – –	– ra – –
Ṡ Ṙ Ġ ,	Ṙ Ṡ N , ।	P M– R G	R S Ṇ S ॥
nan – – –	– – ne –	lu – kō –	– – ra –

Mukthayi Swaram

R , G R	S , Ṇ ,	, R S Ṇ–	P̣ Ṃ P̣ Ṇ ।
S R G S	, S– R M ।	P N D M	R G R S ॥

R M P N , P M–P N Ṡ ,– Ṙ Ġ Ṙ Ṡ N |

Ṙ N , P M P D N | P , M–R , G R S ||

(Indu)

Charanam

N , Ṡ ,– , , P Ṡ– N P , M– R G R S |

Nee – Sa – – – ti – evva – – – ru – – –

Ṇ S· R G– R S R M | P N , S– N P M P ||

nnā – – – ru – – i dha – – ra lo – na –

Chittai Swaras

1. N , P , , , M , , , R , G , R , |

S , Ṇ , , , Ṗ , | Ṇ , S , , R M P ||

(Nee)

2. N Ṡ Ṙ Ṡ , N P D– N P , M– R G R S |

Ṇ Ṗ Ṇ S – R M P | N , Ṙ Ġ– Ṙ S N P ||

(Nee)

3. N P M R G S R G– Ṇ S R S– Ṇ Ṗ Ṇ S |

R G R S R–Ṇ S R | M P N–Ṡ Ṙ Ṡ N P ||

(Nee)

4. S P ,– M P N P M– R G R S ,– S Ṇ Ṗ |

G R , Ṇ– S R P M | , N P Ṡ N P M P ||

N Ṡ Ṙ Ġ , Ṙ– Ṗ Ṁ Ṙ Ġ , Ṙ – Ṡ N P N |

Ṡ Ṙ Ġ Ṡ , N–P M | R G , R S R M P ||

(Nee)

3. PALUMĀRU NINNE KORINA

Ragam : DEVAMANOHARI — 22nd Kharaharapriya Janyam
Talam : ADI
Arohanam : S R_2 M_1 P D_2 N_2 $\dot{S}$
Avarohanam : $\dot{S}$ N_2 D_2 N_2 P M_1 R_2 S
Pallavi : Palumāru Ninne Korina Nāto
Palukavademira Nā Sāmi
Anupallavi : Ilalo Velayu Śri Seshāchala Nivāsa
Śri Venkateśā
Charanam : Nee Sātevvarunnaru Nā Sāmi

3. पलुमारु निन्नेकोरिन

राग : देवमनोहरि
तालम् : आदि

पल्लवि

पलुमारु निन्नेकोरिन नातो
पलुकवदेमिरा ना सामि॥

अनुपल्लवि

इललो वेलयु श्री शेषाचल
निवास श्री वेंकटेश

चरणं

नी साटेव्वरुन्नारु ना सामि

Pallavi

P , M ,–	R , , ,	S S R R–	M M R R |
Pa – lu –	mā – – –	ru – – –	Nin – – –

S Ṇ Ḍ Ṇ– S R M R | M P M R , S R M |
ne – – – Ko – ri – na – nā – to – – – ||

P M R S R M P D– R M P D , N Ṡ N |
Pa – lu – ka – – – va – dē – – – – –

D N P M– R , , S | Ṇ Ḍ Ṇ , , S R M ||
mi – – – ra – – – Na – – – Sā – mi –

Anupallavi

P P M M P–R M P Ṇ S R M– R P M R |
Ila – – – lo – – – ve – la – – – – –

M P D–R M P D N | S R M P– D , N Ṡ ||
yu – – Śri – – – – Śe – – – ṣha – – –

Ṙ Ṙ Ṡ Ṡ– N Ṡ Ṙ Ṁ– Ṙ Ṁ Ṙ Ṡ ,– N D N |
cha – – la Ni – – – Va – – sa – – – –

Ṡ Ṙ Ṁ Ṙ , Ṡ–N D | N P , M– R S R M ||
Śri – – Ven – – ka – te – – – śa – – –

Mukthayi Swaram

P M R S , R– Ṇ S R M , R P M R S |
R M P D ,– N P M | R S R M– P D , , ||
N D N P , M–P D N Ṡ , Ṙ Ṁ Ṙ Ṡ N |
Ṡ Ṙ Ṁ–N Ṡ Ṙ– D N | Ṡ N D N– P M R M ||

(Palumāru)

Charanam

N , , ,– , , Ṡ N– D N P M– R S Ṇ Ḍ |
Nee – – – – – Sa – te – vva – ru – – –

Ṇ S R M , M–R M | P M ,– S R M P D ||
nna – – – – – ru – Nā – – sā – mi – –

Chittai Swaras

1. N , , P , , M , , , R , S , Ṇ , |
Ḍ , Ṇ , , , , S , | R , M , P , , D ||
(Nee)

2. N D N P , M–P M R S , R S Ṇ Ḍ Ṇ |
, S Ṇ S– R M , R | P M R S– R M P D ||
(Nee)

3. N D N P M R S– M R M R S Ṇ Ḍ Ṇ Ṗ |
Ḍ Ṇ S– M R S– P M | R S– N P M R S R ||
(Nee)

4. Ṡ , , , , , N D– N Ṡ N– D N P M R |
M , , , , , P M | R S , R– M P D N ||

Ṡ , N D N P M– P M R S Ṇ Ḍ– Ṇ S R |
M , R S R– M P D | Ṇ S R M– P D N Ṡ ||

Ṡ Ṙ Ṁ Ṙ , Ṙ– R M P M , M– S R M P |
D N– Ṇ S R M P D | Ṇ S R M P D N Ṡ ||

Ṡ , Ṙ Ṁ , Ṙ Ṡ N D– N Ṡ Ṙ Ṡ N D N |
P M M M– R S R , | Ṁ Ṙ Ṁ Ṙ– Ṡ Ṡ N D ||
(Nee)

4. PAGAVĀRI BŌDHANA

Ragam	: HAMSADHWANI – 29th Dheera Śankarabharana Janyam
Talam	: ADI
Arohaṇam	: S R_2 G_3 P N_3 Ṡ
Avarohaṇam	: Ṡ N_3 P G_3 R_2 S
Pallavi	: Pagavāri Bōdhanavini Pantamela Jesevura
Anupallavi	: Pagalureyi Ninneda Bāsi Śri Venkateśwara
Charanam	: Sāmi Neekidi Mera Kādura

4. पगवारि बोधन

राग : हंसध्वनि

तालम् : आदि

पल्लवि

पगवारि बोधन विनि
पंतमेल जेसेवुरा

अनुपल्लवि

पगलुरेई निन्नेड
बासि श्री वेंकटेश्वर

चरणं

सामि नीकिदि मेर कादुरा

Pallavi 8×4 = 32

P , G , R   , , , S   Ṇ S R –   G G R S |
Pa ga – va   – – – ri   – – – –   Bho – – –

S R S S   Ṇ P̣ Ṇ Ṣ | R Ṇ S P   Ṇ S R G ||
dha – – –   na – – –   vi – – ni   – – – –

P P G G R   S–Ṇ Ṇ P̣   G R G –   S   R G P |
Pan – – –   – ta – –   – – – –   me – – –

N Ṡ Ṙ Ṡ   , N P Ṡ | N P , G   R   S R G ||
la – – je   – se – –   – – – vu   –   ra – –

Anupallavi

Ṡ N P P   G R P P   G G R G   S R G P |
Pa – – ga   – – lu –   – – – –   re – yi –

P̣ Ṇ S R   G R S R | G P N P   Ṡ , , , ||
Nin – – –   ne – – –   da – – –   – – – –

S N P Ṙ   , Ṡ Ṅ Ṡ   , Ṙ Ġ Ṗ   Ġ Ṙ Ṡ N |
ba – – si   – – – –   – Śri – –   – – – –

Ġ Ṙ Ṡ N   Ṡ Ṙ Ṡ N | P G R S   Ṇ S R G ||
Ven – – ka   – – te –   – śwa – –   ra – – –

Mukthayi Swaram

P G R S   , Ṇ–G R   S Ṇ , R   S Ṇ–P̣ Ṇ |
P̣ S , Ṇ   R , S G | , R P G   R–S R G ||
P G N P   G–Ṡ N P–   S R G P–   N Ṡ Ṙ Ġ |
Ṗ Ġ Ṙ–N   Ṙ N P Ṙ | Ṡ N P–G   R S R G ||

(Paga)

Charanam

Ṡ , , ,   Ṙ Ṡ N P–   Ṡ N P G–   P G R S |
Sā – – –   mi – – –   Ni – – –   ki – di –

Ṇ S R–G   R S P G ǀ R–Ṡ N P–   G P N N ǁ
Mē – – ra   – – gā –   – du – –   ra – – –

Chittai Swaras

1. Ṡ , , ,   N , , P   , , G ,   R , S , ǀ
R , , Ṇ   , S , , ǀ   , , R G   P , P N ǁ
(Sāmi)

2. Ṡ , , Ṡ   N P–G P   N P , G   R S Ṇ P̣ ǀ
S , , Ṇ   G R S Ṇ ǀ   , S R G   P N Ṡ Ṙ ǁ
(Sāmi)

3. Ṡ N P G   R N P G–   P G R S   Ṇ–G R S ǀ
P̣ S Ṇ G   R–N P G ǀ   Ṡ N P Ġ   Ṙ–Ṗ Ġ Ṙ ǁ
(Sāmi)

4. Ṡ , , Ṡ   , Ṡ–Ṙ Ġ   Ṡ Ṙ , Ṙ   Ṡ N P G ǀ
N , , N   P G R S ǀ   G , , P   G R S Ṇ ǁ
S G P Ṡ   ,– G P N   Ṙ , P N   Ṙ Ġ , Ṙ ǀ
N P Ṡ ,–   N P G S ǀ   ,G P Ṡ ,   – Ṡ R Ġ ǁ
(Sāmi)

5. JALAJĀKṢHI NINNE

Ragam : CHAKRAVAKAM – 16th Melakarta Ragam
Talam : ADI
Arohaṇam : S R_1 G_3 M_1 P D_2 N_2 Ṡ
Avarohaṇam : Ṡ N_2 D_2 P M_1 G_3 R_1 S
Pallavi : Jalajakṣi Ninne Dalachi Dalachi Karuga Chunnadira
Anupallavi : Valarāyuni Kanna Vāsudeva Śri Venkateśa
Charanam : Daya Jesi Dāni nelukorāda

5. जलजाक्षि निन्ने

राग : चक्रवाकम
तालम् : आदि

पल्लवि

जलजाक्षि निन्ने दलचि
दलचि करगुचुन्नदिरा।।

अनुपल्लवि

वल रायुनि कन्न वासुदेव श्री वेंकटेश।।

चरणं

दयचेसि दानि नेलुकोरादा।।

Pallavi 8×4 = 32

G , M ,	G , , ,	M G M G	R R S Ṇ ।
Ja – la –	ja – – –	kshi – nin –	– – – –
S R S S	Ṇ Ḍ Ṇ S ।	Ṇ Ḍ Ṇ Ṗ	Ṗ Ṇ S R ॥
ne – – –	da – – –	la – – chi	– – – –
G M G G	R S P M	G R S M	G M P P ।
Da – la –	Chi – ka –	ra – gu chu	– – – –
N D , D	P M D P ।	, M G R	S Ṇ R G ॥
nna – – di	– – – –	– ra – –	– – – –

Anupallavi

Ṡ Ṡ N N	D P D D	P P M G	M N D N ।
Va – la –	– – ra –	– – yu –	– – – –

P , M D	P M G R |	S R G M	P D N , ||	
ni – – Ka	– – – –	nna – – –	– – – –	
Ṡ N D N	, Ṡ Ṙ Ṡ	N Ṡ Ṙ Ṁ	Ġ Ṙ Ṡ N |	
Va – – –	– su – –	de – – va	– – – –	
D , , N	Ṡ Ṙ Ṡ , |	N D P M	G R S R ||	
Śri – – Ven	– – ka	te – – –	śa – – –	

Mukthāyi Swaram

G M P G	, M R G	S R , R	S Ṇ Ḍ Ṇ |
S R S M	, G M P |	M D P N	D P M , ||
G M P D	, N Ṡ Ṙ	Ġ Ṁ , Ġ	Ṙ Ṡ N D |
N Ṡ Ṙ Ṡ	, Ṙ Ṡ N |	D P , M	G R S R ||

(Jalajakshi)

Charanam

D , N ,	D , , ,	P D N Ṡ	N D P M |
Da – ya –	je – – –	si – – –	Dā – – –
P , , M	G R S Ṇ |	Ḍ , Ṇ S	R G M P ||
ni – – ne	– – lu –	ko – rā –	– da – –

Chittai Swars

1. D , P ,	, , M ,	G , R ,	S , Ṇ , |
Ḍ , Ṇ ,	S , , , |	R , G,	M , P , ||

(Dayajesi)

2. P D N D	, P M P	D P , M	G R S , |
Ṇ Ḍ Ṇ S	, R G M |	P D , N	Ṡ N D P ||

(Dayajesi)

3.	N D P M	G M P D	M G R M	G R S Ṇ ।
	Ḍ Ṇ S R	G M P D ।	N Ṡ N Ṙ	Ṡ N D P ॥

(Dayajesi)

4.	Ṡ , , Ṙ	Ṡ N D ,	N Ṡ N N	D P M G ।
	M , , M	G R S Ṇ ।	S R , G	M P D N ॥
	Ṡ Ṙ Ġ Ṡ	, Ṙ Ġ Ṁ	Ġ , Ṙ Ṡ	N D N Ṡ ।
	Ṙ Ṡ , N	D P , M ।	G R , S	R G M P ॥

(Dayajesi)

6. CHALAMĒLA JĒSĒVU

Ragam : KEERAVĀNI — 21st Melakarta Ragam
Talam : ADI
Arohaṇam : S R_2 G_2 M_1 P D_1 N_3 Ṡ
Avarohaṇam : Ṡ N_3 D_1 P M_1 G_2 R_2 S
Pallavi : Chalamela Jesevu Sāmi Chāla Nammi
Yunna Nāpai
Anupallavi : Palumāru Ninne Korina Nāto
Palukavademi Śri Venkateśa
Charanam : Māruni Bādha korvalera

6. चलमेल जेसेवु

राग : कीरवाणि
तालम् : आदि

पल्लवि

चलमेल जेसेवु सामि
चाल नम्मियुन्न नापै।।

अनुपल्लवि

पलुमारु निन्ने कोरिन
नातो पलुकवदेमि श्री वेंकटेश ॥

चरणं

मारुनि बाध कोर्वलेरा ॥

Pallavi 8×4 = 32

P , M , G R G , R , , S S Ṇ S R |
Cha – la – me – – – la – – je – – – –

G R S Ṇ , Ḍ Ḍ P̣ | Ḍ Ṇ S Ṇ S R G M ||
se – – vu – – – – Sā – – mi – – – –

P M G R G M P , P M P D N , D P |
Cha – – – la – – – Nam – – – mi – – –

D N Ṡ N , D P M | P M G R S R G M ||
yu – – nna – – – – Nā – – – Pai – – –

Anupallavi

P M G R G , M , R G M Ṇ S R G M |
Pa – lu – mā – ru – Nin – – ne – – – –

P M G R G M P D | P M P D N , Ṡ , ||
Kō – – – ri – na – Nā – – – tō – – –

Ṡ N Ṡ Ṙ Ġ Ṙ Ṡ Ṙ N Ṡ N D N D P D |
Pa – lu – – ka – – – va – de – – mi –

Ṡ , N D P , M M | P M G R S R G M ||
Śri – – – ven – kate – – – – – śa – – –

Mukthayi Swaram

P M G R   S , Ṇ S   R G M G   , R S Ṇ |

S R G R   G M P M | G R G M   P , , , ||

P D N D   P D N Ṡ   N , Ṡ Ṙ   Ġ Ṙ Ġ Ṁ |

Ġ Ṙ Ṡ N   D P Ṙ Ṡ | N D P M   G R G M ||

(Chalamela)

Charanam

P , , ,   , , P M   G R G R   S Ṇ Ḍ Ṇ |

Mā – – –   – – ru –   – – ni –   Bā – – –

S , , Ḍ   Ṇ S Ṇ , | S R G R   G M P D ||

dha – – kō   – – rva –   le – – –   ra – – –

Chittai Swaras

1. P , , M   , , G ,   , , R ,   S , Ṇ , |

S , , G   , , R , | G , M ,   P , D , ||

(Maruni)

2. P M D P   , M G R   S Ṇ R S   , Ṇ Ḍ P̣ |

Ḍ Ṇ S Ṇ   , S R G | R G M R   G M P D ||

(Maruni)

3. P D P M   , M G R   G M P M   , G R S |

Ṇ , S R   G R G , | M P D D   P M P , ||

P D P D   N , D P   D N Ṡ ,   N Ṡ Ṙ Ġ |

Ṡ Ṙ Ġ ,   Ṙ Ṡ N D | P M G R   G M P D ||

(Maruni)

4.	N , , ,	, , Ṡ N	D P M G	R S Ṇ Ḍ ।
	Ṇ , , ,	, , Ṡ Ṇ ।	R S G R	G M P D ॥
	N , D P	D N D N	Ṡ N Ṡ ,	, Ṙ Ġ Ṙ ।
	Ġ Ṁ Ġ Ṙ	Ṡ N D , ।	P M G R	G M P D ॥

(Maruni)

7. EVVARI BODHANA

Ragam : ABHOGI – 22nd Kharaharapriya Janyam
Talam : ADI
Arohaṇam : S R_2 G_2 M_1 D_2 Ṡ
Avarohaṇam : Ṡ D_2 M_1 G_2 R_2 S
Pallavi : Evvari bōdhanavini ēlāgu jēsēvurā
Anupallavi : Javvamuga nannēlarā Seshachalendra Śree Venkatēśā
Charanam : Marubāri kōrvajālanurā

7. एव्वरि बोधन

राग : अभोगि
तालम् : आदि

पल्लवि

एव्वरि बोधन विनि
ईलागु जेसेवुरा

अनुपल्लवि

जव्वमुगा नन्नेलरा
शेषाचलेन्द्र श्री वेंकटेश

चरणं

मारु बारि कोर्व जालरा

Pallavi

R , G ,   G R S ,   S R S S   Ḍ Ṃ Ḍ , |

Ev – va –   ri – – –   bō – – –   dha – – –

Ṃ Ḍ S– Ḍ   , S– Ḍ S | R G , – M   G G R S ||

na – – –   – – vi –   – – – ni   – – – –

R G M– G   , M– R G   S R , – Ḍ   S R G M |

I – – –   – – lā –   – – – gu   – – – –

D M D– Ṡ   , Ṡ– D Ṡ | D M ,– G   M G R S ||

jē – – –   – – sē –   – – – vu   – rā – –

Anupallavi

Ṡ Ṡ D– D   , M– D D   M– G , R   G M R G |

Ja – – vva   – – mu –   – ga – –   nan – – –

S R G– M   , M– D M | G R– G M   D D Ṡ , ||

nē – – la   – – ra –   – – Śē –   sha – – –

D Ṡ Ṙ– Ṡ   , Ṙ Ġ Ṁ   Ṙ Ġ ,– Ṁ   Ġ Ġ Ṙ Ṡ |

Cha – – lē   – – ndra –   – – – Śree   – – – –

Ṙ Ġ Ṙ Ṡ   Ṙ– D Ṙ Ṡ | Ṡ D M– D   M G R S ||

Ven – – –   – ka – –   tē – – śwa   rā – – –

Mukthāyi Swaram

R G M– R   , G– S R   G– S , R   S Ḍ Ṃ Ḍ |

S Ḍ S R   ,– R G S | R M , – D   M G R S ||

R G M– G , M– D M D Ṡ ,– Ṙ Ġ Ṡ Ṙ Ġ |

Ṁ Ġ Ṙ– Ġ , Ṙ Ṡ D | Ṙ Ṡ ,– D M G R S ||

(Evva)

Charanam

M , D M D , , , D Ṡ D M D D Ṡ , |
Ma – ru – bā – – – – – – – ri – – –

D Ṡ D D M ,– G M | G R S– R G S R G ||
kō – – – rva – jā – la – – nu – rā – –

Chittai Swarās

1. M , , , , ,– D , M , D , , ,– Ṡ , |
   D , M , , ,– G , | R , S , R , G , ||
   (Maru)

2. M D Ṡ D , M– D M G R ,– G M G R S |
   Ḍ S ,– R G M D Ṡ | ,– D M G R S R G ||
   (Maru)

3. D Ṡ D M G R– G M D M– G R G– S R S |
   R G M D Ṡ– Ṙ Ġ Ṙ | Ṡ D M– G R S R G ||
   (Maru)

4. Ṡ , , –Ṡ , Ṡ– Ṙ Ġ Ṡ Ṙ ,– Ṙ Ṡ D M D |
   Ṡ , ,– Ṡ D Ṙ Ṡ D | ,– Ṡ D M ,– G R S ||
   R G M– D , Ṡ– Ṙ Ġ Ṁ Ṙ ,– Ġ Ṙ Ṡ D Ṡ |
   Ṙ Ṡ ,– D M D– Ṡ D | ,– M G R S , R G ||
   (Maru)

8. ĒRĀNĀPAI

Ragam	: TODI — 8th Hanuma Todi Janyam
Talam	: ADI
Arohaṇam	: S R_1 G_2 M_1 P D_1 N_2 $\dot{S}$
Avarohaṇam	: $\dot{S}$ N_2 D_1 P M_1 G_2 R_1 S
Pallavi	: Erā nāpai inta chauka sēya mērakādurā nā sāmi
Anupallavi	: Māruni kanna Śree Venkatēśā sukumārā nannēlu kōrā sarasudā
Charanam	: Dāni mātalu vini inta sāhasa mēlarā

8. एरानापै

राग : तोडि
तालम् : आदि

पल्लवि

एरा नापै इन्त चौक सेय
मेर गादुरा ना सामि

अनुपल्लवि

मारुनि कन्न श्री वेंकटेश
सुकुमार नन्नेलुकोरा सरसुडा

चरणं

दानि माटलु विनि इन्त साहसमेलरा

Pallavi 8×4 = 32

Ṡ , ,– Ṡ N D–P D N–N D P M G–M N |
Ė – – rā – – nā – – pai – – – – – intha

N D P– M G R S R | G M P– G M P D N ||
caou – – ka – – sē – – – – ya – – – –

Ṡ Ṙ Ġ– N Ṡ Ṙ– D N D– Ġ Ṙ Ṡ N D P M |
Mē – – ra – – kā – – du – – rā – – –

D , , , , ,– Ṡ N | D P M– G M P D N ||
nā – – – – – sā – – – – mi – – – –

Anupallavi

N D D N D D N– G M N D P M G R S |
Mā – – – ru – – ni – kan – – na – – –

M G M– P D N Ṡ N | D P D N Ṡ ,– D P ||
Śree – – Ven – – ka – tē – – – sā – su ku

D N Ṡ Ṙ Ġ Ṙ– Ġ Ṁ Ġ Ṙ– N Ġ Ṙ Ṡ N D
mā – – – rā – nan – – – nē – – – lu –

N Ṡ Ṙ– D N D– Ġ Ṙ | Ṡ N D P M P D N ||
kō – – rā – – sa – ra – su – – dā – –

Mukthāyi Swaram

Ṡ Ṙ Ṡ N D N Ṡ , N Ṙ N– D P M G M |

P D N– D N Ṡ N D | N Ṡ N– Ṙ Ṡ , , , ||

D N D– Ġ Ṙ Ṙ– Ṁ Ġ Ṙ Ṡ– N Ġ Ṙ Ṡ N D |

N Ġ Ṙ– N Ṙ N– D N | D– Ġ Ṙ N D M D N ||

(Erā)

Charanam

D , ,– N Ṙ Ṡ Ṡ N N D P M G R S R ।
Dā – – ni mā – – – ta – – lu – vi ni –

G , ,– M , ,– P D । N Ṡ ,– Ṡ N D P M ॥
in – – ta – – sā – ha sa – mē – la – rā

Chittai Swarās

1. G , ,– M , ,– G , , , R , Ṇ , R , ।
S , ,– Ḍ , ,– Ṇ , । ,– S , R , G , M ॥
(Dāni)

2. D , N D D M– G M D , M– G , R S Ṇ ।
S , R G ,– M D N । Ṡ N ,– D , M G M ॥
(Dāni)

3. M D N Ṡ , N– D N Ṡ N ,– D Ṙ Ṡ N D ।
D , M– G , M N D । M D N Ṡ D , ,– N ॥

D M G R S– D M G R– S R G M D N– Ṡ ।
Ṙ Ġ Ṙ , N– D N D । M G R– Ṇ S R G M ॥
(Dāni)

4. D N D M G M– N D M G R S D M G R ।
S G R Ṇ Ḍ Ṇ R Ṇ । Ḍ Ṇ S R G M D M ॥

D N Ṡ Ṙ N D N Ṡ Ṙ Ġ Ṙ N D N D M ।
G R S– Ġ Ṙ N D M । G R S– Ṇ S R G M ॥
(Dāni)

5. Ṡ , ,– N D N Ṡ , , N– D N N , , D ।
M D N D ,– Ṙ Ṡ N । D , M– G , M D N ॥

Ṙ N D M G R– N D M G R– D M G R S ।
Ṇ S R G M D– S R । G M D– M D N Ṡ Ṙ ॥

Ṡ Ṙ Ġ Ṙ , N– D N Ġ Ṙ , N D N Ṙ N ।
, D– M D N Ṡ , N । D M ,– G M D D N ॥

Ṡ Ṙ Ġ– N Ṡ Ṙ– D N Ṡ– M D N G M D N ।
Ṡ Ṙ Ġ Ṁ Ġ Ṙ– N D । M G R– Ṇ S R G M ॥

(Dāni)

9. VALACHIVACCHI

Ragam : NAVARAGAMALIKA — 9 Rāgās
Talam : ADI
Pallavi : Valachi vacchi yunna nāpai Chalamu sēya mērā sāmi
Anupallavi : Cheluvudaina Sree Venkatēsā Kalasi melasi kougalimcha
Charanam : Pada Sarojamula; Ne Nammiti

9. वलचि वच्चि

राग : नवरागमालिक
तालम् : आदि

पल्लवि (केदार राग)

वलचि वच्चि युन्न नापै
चलमु सेय मेर गादुरा।।

अनुपल्लवि (शंकराभरण राग)

चेलुडैन श्री वेंकटेश
कलसि मेलसि कौगलिंचरा।।

चरणं (कांभोजि राग)

पदसरोजमुल ने नम्मिति।।

Pallavi — Rāgam: KEDARAM 8×4 = 32

P̣ , Ṇ , S , , , S Ṇ S R S S Ṇ Ṇ ।

Va – la – chi – – – va – – – cchi – – –

S M G M P N P P । M M G G R R S Ṇ ॥

yu – – – nna – – – nā – – – pai – – –

P̣ Ṇ S– M G M– P N P– Ṡ N P , M– M G ।

Cha – – la – – mu – – sē – – – ya mē –

R S , , Ṡ N P M । G– N P M G R S Ṇ ॥

– rā – – sā – – – – mi – – – – – –

Anupallavi — Rāgam: SANKARABHARANAM

S , – P , P M G R G , M , P , , , ।

Che – lu – vu – – – dai – – – na – – –

G M P– D D P M P । D N Ṡ N Ṡ , , , ॥

Sree – – Ven – – ka – tē – – – sā – – –

N Ṡ Ġ Ṙ Ṡ N– Ṡ R Ġ ,– Ṁ Ġ Ṙ Ṡ N P ।

ka – la – – – si – – – me – – la – –

N D – Ṡ , ,– M P D । P , ,– – M G R S Ṇ ॥

si – – kou – ga – – lim – – – Cha – – –

Mukthāyi Swaram — Rāgam: KALYANI

Ḍ Ṇ S R   , G–S R   G M ,– D   P M G R |

Ṇ G R– Ṇ   R Ṇ Ḍ Ṇ | S R G M   P , , , ||

D M G R   S ,– Ḍ Ṇ   S R ,– G   , M P D |

G M P D   , N P D | M P D N   Ṡ , , , ||

Rāgam: BEGADA

N D P– M   , G R G   D M ,– G   R S Ṇ Ḍ |

P̣ S ,– Ṇ   R S G R | P M D P   Ṡ N Ṙ Ṡ ||

Ġ Ṙ Ġ M   Ġ Ṁ Ṙ ,   Ṡ N Ṙ Ṡ   Ṙ N D P |

M M ,– G   R S S , | ,– M G G   R– R S Ṇ ||

(Valachi)

Charanam — Rāgam: KAMBOJI

P , D ,   Ṡ ,– Ṡ N   D ,– D N   P , , , |
Pa – da –   sa – rō –   – – – –   ja – – –

M P D– N   N D– P N | D D P– D   P M G M ||
mu – – la   – – Ne –   Nam – –   mi – ti –

Chittai Swaras — Rāgam: YADUKULAKAMBOJI

1. P , ,– M   , ,– G ,   , , R ,   G , R , |
S , ,– P̣   , ,– Ḍ , | , ,– S ,   ,– R , M ||

(Pada)

Rāgam: BILAHARI

2. P D P M   G R G ,   D P M G   R S Ṇ Ḍ |
P̣ Ḍ S R   G P M G | R S R G   P , , , ||

P M G R ,– G P D S ,– R G P D S , |
S R G P D Ṡ– Ḍ S | R G P , M G R G ||

(Pada)

Rāgam: MOHANAM

3\. P , D R G R G , D R G R G P G R |
S , G R S R S , | R S Ḍ S R G P D ||

Ṡ D P G R S– D P G R– S R G P D Ṡ |
Ṙ Ġ Ṙ Ṡ D– P D Ṡ | D P G R S R G G ||

(Pada)

Rāgam: SREE

4\. P , ,– P M R– G , ,– G R S Ṇ S G R |
S , ,– S Ṇ P̣ Ṇ , | ,– S , R ,– M , M ||

P M R G R S– Ṇ S R M P– S R M P N |
P Ṡ N– P , M– R G | R S– R M P N Ṡ , ||

P N Ṡ– Ṙ , Ṙ– N Ṡ Ṙ Ġ ,– Ġ Ṙ Ṡ N Ṡ |
Ġ Ṙ Ġ– Ṡ , Ṙ– Ṙ Ṡ | Ṙ– N , Ṡ P N Ṡ Ṙ ||

Ṙ Ġ ,– Ġ Ṙ Ṡ– N Ṙ ,– Ṙ –Ṡ N P D N P |
M– R G R S ,– Ġ Ṙ | Ṡ N P– Ṙ Ṡ N P M ||

(Pada)

10. ĒRĀNĀPAI

Ragam : MUKHARI — 22nd Mēla Khoraharapriya janyam
Talam : ADI
Arohanam : S R_2 M_1 P N_2 D_2 Ṡ
Avarohanam : Ṡ N_2 D_1 P M_1 G_2 R_2 S

Pallavi	: Erā nāpai intha kōpamēlarā evvari bōdhana vinnāvurā
Anupallavi	: Dheerudaina Sree Subrahmanya rārā nannēlukōrā ĪVēla
Charanam	: Neerajaksha nāpai Daya Yunchara

10. एरानापै

राग : मुखारि
तालम् : आदि

पल्लवि

एरा नापै इन्त कोपमेलरा
एव्वरि बोधन विन्नावुरा।।

अनुपल्लवि

धीरुडैन श्री वेंकटेश
रारा नन्नेलुकोरा ई वेल।।

चरणं

नीरजाक्षा नापै दययुंचरा।।

Pallavi 8×4 = 32

Ṡ , ,– Ṡ	N D– P N	D– D P M	G R M P	I
Ē – – rā	– – nā –	– pai – –	– – in tha	
N D P– M	, M– P M I	G R S– R	M P N D	II
kō – – pa	– – me –	– – – la	– rā – –	
Ṡ N D– P	, M– D P	M– G , R	M G R S	I
ev – – va	– – ri –	– bō – –	dha – – –	

Ṇ Ḍ S R , S– P M ı G , R– S R M P D ıı
na – – vi – – nnā – – – – vu – rā – –

Anupallavi

P , D P M– G , R S R M– G , R S Ṇ ı
Dhee – ru – – dai – – na – – Sree – – – –

Ḍ S R M , G– R M ı P– N , D M P D Ṡ ıı
Su – – bra – – hma – – – – – nya – – –

Ṙ , ,– Ṁ Ġ Ṙ– Ṡ Ṙ Ġ– Ṡ , N D– M P D ı
rā – – rā – – nan – – nē – – – lu – –

Ṡ , ,– N , D– M P ı D M ,– G R M P D ıı
kō – – ra – – – – I vē – – la – – –

Mukthāyi Swaram

Ṡ N ,– D P M– D P ,– M G R M G R S ı
Ḍ S ,– R M G– R P ı , M– N D P– M P D ıı
Ṡ Ṙ Ṁ Ġ ,– Ṡ Ṙ Ġ Ṡ ,– N D P– M P D ı
Ṡ Ṙ Ġ Ṡ ,– N D P ı M G R– S R M P D ıı

(Era)

Charanam

N , ,– D , ,– Ṡ N D P , M G R P M ı
Nee – – ra – – jā – – – – ksha nā – – –

P , , , , ,– P M ı G R S– R , M P D ıı
pai – – – – – da – ya – – yun – cha – ra

Chittai Swarās

1. N , ,– D , ,– P , M , ,– G , , R , |
S , ,– Ṇ , ,– Ḍ , | S , ,– R , M P D ||
(Nee)

2. N D P M , G–R M P D ,– N D Ṡ N D |
Ṙ Ṡ ,– Ġ Ṙ Ṡ N D | P M ,– G R M P D ||
(Nee)

3. P D M P M G R–S R P M G R S Ṇ D |
S R M G R–R D P | Ṡ N D–Ṙ Ṡ Ġ Ṙ Ṡ ||
(Nee)

4. D P ,– M G R– S R ,– P M G R S Ṇ Ḍ |
S Ḍ ,– S R G S , | R P M G R M P D ||
Ṡ Ṙ Ṁ Ġ , Ṙ– Ṡ Ṙ Ṡ N , D P M P D |
P Ṡ ,– N D P ,– M | G R ,– S R M P D ||
(Nee)

8

Ata Tala Varnams of Patnam Subramanya Iyer

(Lyrics with Notation)

PADA VARNAM

1. SAMINI VEGAME

Ragam	:	NATAKURANJI – 28th Harikambhoji Janyam
Talam	:	Khandajati Ata Talam
Arohanam	:	S R_2 G_3 M_1 N_2 D_2 N_2 P D_2 N_2 $\dot{S}$
Avarohanam	:	$\dot{S}$ N_2 D_2 M_1 G_3 S : $\dot{S}$ N_2 D_2 M_1 G_3 M_1 P G_3 R_2 S
Pallavi	:	Sāmini Vegame Rammanave Sārasākshiro Ivela Nā ‖
Anupallavi	:	Srimānyudaina Srikota Sāmi Bhupāluni Chennu Dalachi Marulaitini
Muktāyi Swara Sāhityam	:	Nammikagala Cheli Nee–vani Ninu Nammiti Namma Komma nimmalamuga Paliki Marmamu Telusukōrammipudu Pommu Samayamu Ramātanayudēyu Virisaramulu Karamulanduriyuchu Nā yuramuna Tagili Duramuganu Nādu Ichchenaka

Migula Nochchitinani Telipi
(Samini Vegame)

Charanam : Daya Jēsi Nannelukommanave Nāpai

Chittai Swara Sahityas :

1. Mannana jēsi Sanudenchi Nanu
   Raminchutakidi Manchi Samayamipudu ॥
   (Daya Jesi)
2. Cheluva Gunamu Vadali Yalla Kaluvalare dalaru Viltudu Tana Yalludanu Nepamu Valana Vibhākaruni Vale Vēdimi Gunamunu Chēkone Nipudu ॥ (Daya Jesi)
3. Karamativaku Maru Neeyeda Nerigiyalaru Sarani Narasi Chirukaru—Valivirahulidumulu Pada Tana Saravadiyagu Manaluvale birabiravisaradonake Nipudu ॥ (Daya Jesi)
4. Sōkkapu paruvamu Balsakkadanamu Mariyekkuvagu Chaturathanu Pikkadilina Yekkatikamana Sakala vibhuni Yedabāsi Yetulu Manasu Nilpudunu Nimishamu Yokka yugamugānu Talapukonuchu Nalasitini Tālanika Tāmasamu Salupakanu Nā Manavini Telipi Cheluvuni (Daya Jesi)

1. सामिनि वेगमे (पद वर्णम)

राग : नटकुरन्जि

तालम् : खंडजाति अटतालम

पल्लवि

समिनि वेगमे रम्मनवे
सारसाक्षिरो ई वेल ना।।

अनुपल्लवि

श्रीमान्युडैन श्रीकोट सामि
भूपालुनि चेन्नु दलचि मरुलैतिनि।।

मुक्ताइ स्वर साहित्यम

नम्मिकगल चेलि नीवनि
निनु नम्मिति नम्म कोम्मनिम्मलमुगा
पलिकि मर्ममु तेलुसुकोरम्मिपुड्डु
पोम्मु समयमु रमा तनयुडेयु
विरिसरमुलु करमुलंदुरियुचु
ना युरमुन तगिलि
दुरमुगनु नाडु इच्चेनक
मिगुल नोच्चितिननि तेलिपि।। (सामिनि वेगमे)

चरणं

दयजेसि नन्नेलुकोम्मनवे नापै।

चिट्टैस्वर साहित्य

1. मन्नन जेसि सन्नुदेंचि ननु
रमिंचुटकिदि मन्चि समयमिपुड्डु।। (दयजेसि)

2. चेलुव गुणमु वदलि यल्ल कलुवलरे
डलरू विल्तुड्डु तन यल्लुडनु नेपमु
वलन विभाकरुनि वले वेडिमि
गुणमु चेकोने निपुड्डु।। (दयजेसि)

3. करमतिवकु मरु नीयेड
नेरिगियलरु सरनि नरसि
चिरूकरू वलिविरहलिड्डुमुलु पडतन
शरवडियगु मनलुवले
बिरबिरवि शरदोनके निपुड्डु।। (दयजेसि)

4. शोक्कपु परुवमु बलसक्कदनमु
मरिएक्कूवगु चतुरतनु
पिक्कटिलिनयेक्कटि कमन
सकल विभुनि एडबासि।
एट्टुलु मनसु निलपुदुनु निमिषमु।
ओक्क युगमुगानु तलपुकोनुचु।
नलसितिनि तालनिक तामसमु।
सलुपकनु ना मनविनि तेलिपि चेलुवुनि।। (दयजेसि)

Pallavi 14×4 =56

, , , , , , , , M , G ,– S , , Ṇ– Ḍ , N , I
– – – – – – – – Sa – – – mi– – – – – – –

S ṆS ,– S , , , Ṇ S R G– M MG M R G R S I
ni – – – – – – – Ve – – – ga – – me – – – –

Ṇ S G R S Ṇ–R S I Ṇ–S Ṇ Ḍ– N S Ḍ Ṇ II
Ram – – – – – – – ma– – – – – – –

P̣ ḌP̣–Ḍ Ṇ S R G M MG G S–G S–M G S ṆḌ I
na – – Ve – – – – Sā – – – – – – ra – – – –

Ṇ S R G M–S MG– M ND–N Ṡ ND N– P D NṠ I
sa – – – – – – – kshi – – – – – – ro– – –

N DN , ,– N D M I M , , G M G S R II
– – – – – I – – Ve – – la – – nā–

Anupallavi

Ṇ S Ṇ–Ḍ ṆS R G*S , Ṡ N NṠ N D– M G MN I
– – – – – – – – Sri – – mān – – – – yu– – –

N D M–D MM G S M , G M R S Ṇ–Ḍ Ṇ S R G |
dai – – na – – – – Sri – – – – – – ko – ta – –

S , ,– R G M N , | D , N–P D N Ṡ N ||
Sā – – mi – – – – Bhū – – pā – – – –

D D N N– Ṡ , , , Ṡ ND N– Ṡ Ṙ Ġ Ṡ , Ṙ Ġ Ṁ |
lu – – – ni – – – Chen – – – – – – – – nu – –

Ṁ Ġ–Ṡ Ṙ Ṙ Ṡ N D N Ṡ Ṙ– N Ṡ D N–P D N D M |
– – – – – – – – da – – la – – – chi – – – –

G M N N D N–P D | N Ṡ , N– D M G M ||
Ma – ru – – – lai – – – – – ti – – –

M G S– S Ṇ S R G
– – – ni – – – – –

Muktāyi Swara Sahityam

, , , , , , , , M , G S R S–Ṇ R S , Ṇ Ḍ |
– – – – – – – – Na mmi Kagala Cheli Nee Vani

Ṇ S Ṇ , Ḍ Ṇ– P̣ , Ṇ Ḍ , Ṇ– S , Ṇ Ḍ Ṇ S R G |
Ninu Nam miti Namma Komma ni mmalamuga paliki

S , M , M–G G S | N D ,– D M G M , ||
ma r ma mu telusu Kora mmi pudu Po

G S Ṇ S R G M , M M G S , N N D M G S , |
mmu sa maya mu ra mā ta na yu de yu viri sa ra mu lu

R G M G , M– N D N P , D–N Ṡ Ṙ Ġ Ṁ Ġ Ṡ N |
Ka ra mu la – n du ri yu chu Nā yu ra mu na Tagilidura

Ṡ Ṙ N Ṡ , N– D N I Ṡ , , Ṡ N D M , ||
mu ga nu Nā du Ichche naka – Mi gu la no

, M G Ṣ Ṇ– S R G
– Chchitinani Telipi (Sāmini Vegame)

Charanam

, , , ,– , , , , D , N ,– D , , ,– N D N Ṡ I
– – – – – – – – Da– ya– je – – – si – – –

N N D D M , , ,– M G M N N D M–G M G S Ṇ I
Nan– – – ne– – – – – – – – – – lu – – – –

S R S M– G M N D I N P D N Ṡ , , Ṡ ||
Ko– mma– na– – – ve– – – Nā– – pai

Chittai Swara Sahityas

1. M , , , , , M , ,–G , S , , , N , Ḍ , Ṇ I
Man na na Je si Sanuden

S , , ,– , , S , , Ṇ , Ḍ ,–Ṇ P̣ , , , Ḍ , I
chi Na nu ra minchu ta

Ṇ , S , R , S , I , , D ,– M , G , ||
kidi manchi Sa ma ya

S , R , G , M ,
mi – pu – – – du – (Daya Jēsi)

2. N N D M G S– M M G S , Ṇ Ḍ Ṇ S R S , , , I
Che lu va Gu na mu Va da li ya lla ka lu va la re

Ṇ Ḍ Ṇ S , Ṇ – S R S M , G – M N D N P D N Ṡ |
da la ru vi litu du tana ya llu da nu ne pa mu va la na

N Ṙ , Ṡ N D – N Ṡ | N , , D N – P D N ‖
vibhā ka runi Vale vē di mi Gu na mu

D M , G– S R G M
nu chē ko ne ni pu du (Daya Jēsi)

3. Ṡ N D M G S– N D M G S– D M G S– M G S Ṇ Ḍ |
Ka ra ma ti va ku ma ru nee yeda Neri gi ya laru Sarani

Ṇ S R– S M G– M N D N– Ṡ N D N– P D N Ṡ Ṙ G |
Na rasi chi ru ka ru va li vi ra hu li du mu lu pa da ta na

Ṁ Ġ Ṁ Ṙ Ġ Ṡ– N Ṙ | Ṡ N D– N Ṡ N D M ‖
Sa ra va di ya gu na na lu va le – bi ra bi ravi

N D M G S– R G M
sa ra do na ke Nipudu (Daya Jēsi)

4. S M M G S N S R S , , , S , R S N D Ṇ S |
so kka pu pa ru va mu Bal sa kkada namu Ma ri

Ṇ , , Ḍ Ṇ P̣ Ḍ Ṇ– S R G S , S– R G M G , M |
ye kku vagu chatu ra tha nu Pikkadi li na ye kka

R G M R– S Ṇ Ḍ Ṇ | S R S M M , , , ‖
ti ka ma na sakala vi bhu ni Ye da bā

M G M R G S– N N S M G S– M G M D N Ṡ– Ṙ Ġ |
si ye tu la Ma na su ni lu pu du nu Nimishamu yokkayuga

Ṁ Ṙ , Ġ Ṡ Ṙ N Ṡ , Ṙ Ṡ N– D N Ṡ N , D M G I
mu gā nu Tala pu kon chu na la sitini Tāla ni ka

S , ,– R G M D N I Ṡ Ṁ Ġ Ṡ ,– N D M II
Tā ma sa mu Sa lu pa ka nu Nā Ma na vi

G S ,– Ṇ S R G M
ni Te li pi chelu vu ni (Daya Jēsi)

2. MANASĒTIKI

Ragam : SĀVERI — 15th Mayamalava Goula Janyam
Talam : Khandajati Ata Talam
Arohanam : S R_1 M_1 P D_1 Ṡ
Avarohanam : Ṡ N_3 D_1 P M_1 G_3 R_1 S
Pallavi : Manasetiki Karagadu Rāma
Māninі Yenta Vedukonnagāni
Anupallavi : Vinarā Sri Venkateswara
Velasi Nāpai Neramemira Delupura
Charanam : Mārubariki Tāla Jaalanura

2. मनसेटिकि

राग : सावेरि

तालम् : खंडजाति अट तालम्

पल्लवि

मनसेटिकि करगदु रामा
मानिनि एन्त वेडुकोन्न गानि।।

अनुपल्लवि

विनरा श्री वेंकटेश्वरा
वेलसि नापै नेरमेमिरा देलुपुरा।।

चरणं

मारुबारिकि तालजालनुरा।।

Pallavi 14×4 = 56

, , , , , , , , * M , M ,– G , , R– R , , , |
Ma na se – –

R R P M– G R S ,– R G G R S G R S ṆḌP̣Ḍ |
ti – – – – – – – ki – – – – Ka – – – ra – –

R R S–Ḍ S R M G | R M P D M , P M ‖
– – – ga – – – – – du – – – – Ra –

G R S–Ḍ , R S R M P D D M G R S ,– R M P |
– – – ma – – – – Ma – – – ni – – – – ni – –

D P D M ,– P DṠ– M P DṠ , N D P– D M , G |
En – – – – tha – – ve – – – – du – – ko – – –

R S–G R , S ṆḌ | , S R M P D P M ‖
– – nna – – – – – – ga – – – ni – –

Anupallavi

R , , S R–ḌS R , M P D D P D – M D P G R |
– – – – – – – – Vi – na – – – – rā – – – –

M P D P , M–P D N P , P– D N P D ,– M P M |
Sri – – – – – – – – – – – Ven – – – ka – –

D P ,– N D P–D M | G R S–Ḍ S R M P ‖
te – – – – – swa – – – – ra – – – –

DMPD Ṡ , , , D , D, SṘĠ, ĠṘṠṘ |
– – – – – – – – Va – la – si – – – – – – –

Ṁ , Ṁ, Ġ, Ġ, Ṙ ṠṘĠ Ṙ–Ṡ ĠṘ ṠṘ , D |
Pai – – – – – – – Ne – – – ra – – – – – – –

Ṙ ṠND P–M P D | Ṡ , , N DP–DN ||
me – – – – mi – – ra – – Te – – – –

DMGR SḌSR
lu – pa – – ra – –

Mukthayi Swaram

, , , , , , , , M, P, D–MDP GR–PM |

P , P,– SRR–D P , DM ,– PMG RSṆḌ |

RS ,–Ḍ SRPM | DPND PMGR ||

MPDN D, , , PDṠṘ , ĠṠṘ Ṁ , ĠṘ |

Ṡ , ṘĠ Ṡ ,–Ṙ Ġ ṘṠṘ,– DṘṠN D–MPD |

ṠṘĠṠ , NDP | DMGR SĠṘN ||

DMGR S–ḌS R (Manasetiki)

Charanam

, , , , , , , , M , M ,– P DM D PMGR
– – – – – – – – Mā – ru – bā – – – – – – –

MPDM P, , ,– M PDN D ,–P N DP MP |
ri – – – – – – – ki – – – – – Tha – – – – – –

DDMG RS–MG | R SṆḌ S , , , ||
la – – – – – ja – la – nu – ra – – –

Chittai Swaras

1. D , , ,– , , P ,– , , D ,– P , M ,– , , D , |

P , M ,– G , R ,– , , P ,– M , G ,– R , S , |

, , Ḍ ,– S , R , | M , P ,– , , M , ‖

G , R ,– S , R , (Mārubāriki)

2. D , P M GR– P , MGRM , G RS ṆḌṚ , |

S , , Ḍ S R MP ,– D P N DP ,– M P D Ṡ Ṙ |

Ġ Ṙ , Ṡ ND– Ṡ , | , Ṙ ND P M– D M ‖

GRS– Ḍ , R S R (Mārubāriki)

3. Ṡ N D– P D MP D– N DP D MGR S GRS , |

ṆḌR S– MGR– P MDP D– MPD– Ṡ NDṘṠ |

ĠṘṠ N– DPMP | DṠ Ṙ– P DṠN D ‖

PMG R S– ḌS R (Mārubāriki)

4. M , ,– M GRS R M ,– , G RḌS R M ,– , D |

P MGR M , ,– Ṡ NDPD M ,– , D P DṠ Ṙ |

Ṁ , ,– Ġ Ṙ Ṡ N D | M , ,– G R S ṆḌ ‖

Ṃ , ,– Ḍ P̣ ḌS R (Mārubāriki)

5. S R S– P , M G R S R– MM , G R S ṆḌR , |

S , ,– Ḍ S R Ḍ ,– S R G S ,– R MP R ,– MP |

D M ,– G R S ṆḌ | S R MP D ,– , , ‖

Ṡ N D P ,– D MG R M P D– Ṡ Ṙ Ġ Ṡ , Ṙ Ṁ Ṁ |

, Ġ Ṙ Ṡ N D P M– P D Ṡ Ṙ , Ṙ–M P D Ṡ , Ṡ |

R M P–D , D–Ṡ Ṙ | Ġ Ṙ ,– Ġ Ṙ Ṡ N D ||

P–M G R S–Ḍ S R (Mārubāriki)

3. IKANĒLANE

Ragam : PURNACHANDRIKA —
29th Dheera Sankarabharana janyam

Talam : Khandajati Ata Talam

Arohanam : S R_2 G_3 M_1 P D_2 P Ṡ

Avarohanam : Ṡ N_3 P M_1 R_2 G_3 M_1 R_2 S

Pallavi : Ikanelane Vānito Chelimi
Intiro chālu Pommanave

Anupallavi : Ākata Nannilāgu Mōsamu Jēsina
Ādi Venkateswarudu Gādate

Charanam : Pagavāri Bhodhana Vinna Vāde kadā

3. इकनेलने

राग : पूर्णचन्द्रिक

तालम् : खंडजाति अट तालम्

पल्लवि

इकनेलने वानितो चेलिमि
इन्तिरो चालु पोम्मनवे

अनुपल्लवि

आकट नन्निलागु मोसमु
जोसिन आदि वेंकटेश्वरूडु गादडे

चरणं

पगवाारि भोधन विन्नवाडे कदा।।

Pallavi 14×4 = 56

, , , ,– , , , , G , M ,– P , , ,– P MP M |
Ika ne – – – – – – – – – –

R , , ,– G M P P MR– P M R G M R– S R S S |
la – – – ne – – – – – Vā – – – – – ni – – –

Ṇ P̣– ḌR S R , R | G M P– R G M P– D ||
to – – – – – – – Che – – li – – – –

P , M,– G M R S R– G M P P M R– G M P M P |
mi – – – – – – – – In – – – – ti – – – –

P M R G M P D,– P Ṡ , Ṡ N P D P , M G M |
ro – – – – – – – Chā – – – – – lu – – – – –

Ṙ Ṡ , Ṡ N P– D Ṙ | Ṡ Ṙ– G M M P R , ||
Pom – – – – – ma – na – Ve – – – – –

Anupallavi

P M G M R S R , Ṡ Ṡ N N P M– P M G M R G |
– – – – – – – – Aā – Ka – – – ta – – – – –

M P D P , M P Ṡ N P , M R G M R , S Ṇ P , |
Na – – nni – la – – – – – gu – – – – – – – – –

Ḍ R S R G M– R G | M P M R– S R G M |
Mō – sa – – – mu – je – – – – – – –

P D P Ṡ– Ṡ , , , Ṡ N P Ṙ , Ṙ– Ṡ Ṙ Ġ Ṁ Ṙ , |
si – – – na – – – Ā – – di – Ven – – – – – –

Ṗ Ṁ Ġ Ṁ Ṙ , Ṡ N– P Ṙ Ṡ Ṡ N P– M D P P M R |

ka – – – – – – – – te – – – – – swa – – – –

G M P– R G M– S R | G M – P D P Ṙ Ṡ ||

ru – – – – – du – – – – ga – – – –

N P M– G M R S R

da – – te – – – –

Muktayi Swaram

, , , , , , , , G , M P M R– G M R S Ṇ P̣ |

R , R– P Ṡ , Ṡ– P M R G , G– S R G M P M R |

G M P D , P Ṡ N | P , M– G M R S R ||

G M P D P , , , P M R G , M P D– P Ṡ , Ṡ |

Ṙ Ṡ Ṙ Ġ , Ṁ– Ṙ Ġ Ṁ Ṙ , Ṡ– Ṡ Ṙ Ṡ Ṡ N P– P M |

G M R G– M P D P | Ṙ Ṡ – Ṡ N P– Ṡ RN ||

P , M– G M R S R (Ikanēlane)

Charanam

, , , , , , , , P , P , Ṡ , , , Ṡ N P , |

Pa – ga – va – – – – – – –

D , , , Ṡ N P M G M R ,– S R G M P M– G M |

ri – – – bō – – – – dha – na – – – – – – –

P ,– P Ṡ N P– Ṙ , | Ṡ , ,– Ṙ Ṡ N P– Ṡ ||

vi – nna – – – – Va – – de – ka – da

Chittai Swaras

1. P , , M , , G , , , M,– R , S ,– N, P, ।
R , , ,– , , R , G , M , , R , S ,– Ṇ, P̣ ।
S , , ,– , , Ṡ , । N , P , M , G , ॥
M , R ,– G , M , (Paga Vāri)

2. P , DP– Ṡ NP M– P , , D P MGM RS ṆP̣ ।
S , , P MRG ,– MPD–P Ṡ , Ṡ–Ṙ ĠṀṘṠ ।
Ṙ , Ṡ , Ṡ NP–D । ,P , MG M– RS ॥
ṆP̣RS ,– RGM (Paga Vāri)

3. ṠṠ N–P DPṠ N– PMR–G PMR G– MRSR ।
SRG M– PMR–S RGMP– Ṡ NP–Ṙ Ṡ ṘĠṀ ।
ṖṀṘ– Ġ ṀṘṠ N । PMR–G MRS Ṇ ॥
P̣RS– P MRGM (Paga Vāri)

4. S R G , M–R GM P , MR– GMRS ṆP̣– R , ।
S , , , , ,– S Ṇ P̣ Ḍ ,– R SRGM R ,– PM ।
R ,– D P M R , G । MP–S R GMP , ॥
P D P Ṡ , N–PṠ , Ṡ NP– DP , M GM–RG ।
MP–Ṡ Ṡ , Ṡ ṠṠ । PP , R R , GM ॥
Ṙ Ṡ N–P M R GM (Paga Vāri)

4. PADAREDI

Ragam : YADUKULA KĀMBHOJI — 28th Harikambhoji Janyam
Talam : Khandajati Ata Talam
Arohanam : S R_2 M_1 P D_2 N_2 D_2 P D_2 Ṡ

Avarohanam : Ṡ N_2 D_2 P M_1 G_3 R_2 S
Pallavi : Padarēdi Meragādura
Bhāmāmanipai Nēramēmira
Aṇupallavi : Sadayudaina Sri Venkateswara
Sāmānyula mātalella vini
Charanam : Panati Ninne Nammiyunnadira

4. पदरेदि

राग : यदुकूलकांभोजि
तालम् : खंडजाति अट तालम्

पल्लवि

पदेरदि मेर गादुरा
भामामणिपै नेरमेमिरा।।

अनुपल्लवि

सदयुडैन श्री वेंकटेश्वरा
सामान्युल माटलेल्ला विनि।।

चरणं

पणति निन्ने नम्मियुन्नदिरा।।

Pallavi 14×4 = 56

, , , ,– , , , , P̣ , Ḍ , S , , Ṇ– S , R S ।
Pada – re – – – – – – –

R , , ,– R , , , S R M M G R– R M G G R S ।
di – – – – – – – Me – – – – – ra – – – – –

S S R– S , R– S R । M M G S ,– R P M ॥
ka – – – – – – – – – – – – – – du –

, G– R M   G G R S   S R M M   G– M P M–   G M P , ।
ra – – –   – – – –   Bhā – –   – – – –   – – – –

M P M– D   D P– M P   M M G R–   R M G R   , G R S ।
mā – – –   – – ma –   – – – –   pai – –   – – – –

Ṡ P ,– D   Ṡ N Ṡ , । R M G S   R , , D ॥
Nē – – –   – – ra –   mē – – –   mi – – ra

Anupallavi

D P P M   G G R S   D , D ,   P , , ,–   M P D P ।
– – – –   – – – –   Sa da   yu – – –   dai – –

D Ṡ Ṡ N   D N D P–   D D M P   , M– P D   P P M G ।
– – – na   – – – –   Sri – –   – – Ven   – – – –

M P M G   R– G R S । R M G– M   P M– P D ॥
ka – – –   – te – –   swa – –   – – ra –

P– M P D   Ṡ , , ,   P D Ṡ Ṡ   , Ṙ Ṡ Ṙ   Ġ Ṡ , Ṙ ।
– – – –   – – – –   Sā – – –   – mā – –   – – – –

Ṙ Ṁ Ġ Ṙ   , Ġ Ṙ Ṡ   Ṙ Ṙ Ṡ Ṡ   , Ṡ– Ṡ N   D D P M ।
nyu – –   – la – –   ma – – –   – – – –   – – – –

P D Ṡ N   , D P N । D P , M–   D P M P
ta – – –   – le – –   – – – –   lla – –

P M G R   M G R S
Vi – – ni   – – – –

Mukthayi Swaram

, , , ,   , , , ,   P̣ , Ḍ Ḍ   , S– P̣ ,   Ḍ S , R ।
S R G S–   R , R ,   R M G ,–   R G R R   , G R S ।
S S R S   , R– M M । P M , G–   R M G R ॥
S R M M   P , , ,   D D P P   M G– R M   G S R M ।
P D Ṡ Ṙ–   Ṡ Ṙ Ġ Ṙ–   Ṁ Ṙ Ġ Ṙ–   Ṁ Ġ Ṙ Ṡ   , Ṙ Ṡ N ।
D P ,– D   P M P D । Ṙ Ṡ , N   D P D P ॥
, M G R   , G R S   (Padaredi)

Charanam

, , , ,   , , , ,   P , P ,   P M G ,–   R M G S ।
Pa – na –   thi – –   – – – –

R , P M   P , , ,–   M P D P   , D– M P   D Ṡ D P ।
Nin – –   – – – –   ne – – –   – – Nam   – – mi –

M D P P   , M– G M । P– P M G–   R M G R ॥
yu – – nna   – –   – –   di – – –   ra – – –

Chittai Swaras

1. P , , ,   , , P ,–   M , G ,–   , , M ,–   P , M , ।
G , R ,–   , , R ,–   M , G ,–   R , S ,   , , P , ।
Ḍ , S ,–   , , R , । M , G ,–   , , R , ॥
G , S ,   R , M ,   (Panati)

2. P , N D   P– M P D   P , , D   M D P– P   , M G R ।
R M G R   ,– G R S–   R M G M   ,– P D P–   M P D Ṡ ।

Ṙ Ṡ ,– Ṡ N D N D I D P M– P D Ṡ P , ||
M G , R ,– S R M (Panati)

3. P D P P M G– M P M M G R– R M G R G S R S I
R M G M P M– P D P– D Ṡ N N D P– D P M P D I
Ṡ Ṙ Ṁ Ṁ Ġ Ṙ– Ṡ Ṙ I Ġ Ġ Ṙ Ṡ N D– Ṙ Ṡ ||
N D P M G S R M (Panati)

4. S R P M , G– R M G , , R– S R G S R S , , I
S P̣ ,– Ḍ S R S , R– M G S R,– R P M , G S I
R M P D P ,– M G I R S R M P , , , ||
M P D Ṡ , D– Ṡ Ṙ Ṁ , Ġ Ṙ , Ġ Ṙ Ṡ– D Ṙ Ṡ Ṡ I
N D– P N D D P M– P D Ṡ Ṙ , Ṙ– M P D Ṡ , Ṡ I
N D P– M P D P , I M G R– S R G S , ||
Ṡ N N D– D P P M (Panati)

5. EVAREMI

Ragam	: SAHANA — 28th Harikambhoji Janyam
Talam	: Khandajati Ata Talam
Arohanam	: S R_2 G_3 M_1 P M_1 D_2 N_2 Ṡ
Avarohanam	: Ṡ N_2 Ṡ D_2 P M_1 G_3 M_1 R_2 G_3 R_2 S
Pallavi	: Evaremi Bhodhana Jesināro Yemo Nēnetlā Telpudunammā
Anupallavi	: Jāvaraliro Vinave Sri Seshāchalendrudaina Sri Venkateswaruniki
Charanam	: Palumāru Ne Pilichina Raadēmi Sētune

5. एवरेमि

राग : शहन
तालम् : खंडजाति अट तालम्

पल्लवि

एवरोमि भोधन जेसिनारो
एमो ने नेट्‌ल तेलुपुदुनम्मा।।

अनुपल्लवि

जावरालिरो श्री शेषाचलेन्द्रुडैन
श्री वेंकटेश्वरूनिकि।।

चरणं

पलुमारु ने पिलचिना राडेमि सेतुने।।

Pallavi 14×4 = 56

, , , ,– , , , , R , R ,– G M P ,– P M G M |
Eva – – re – – – – – – –

R , G R S , , , Ṇ S Ṇ G R S R S– Ṇ S Ṇ Ḍ |
mi – – – – – – – Bhō – – – – – – dha – –

Ḍ Ṇ Ḍ Ḍ P̣ Ṃ–Ḍ , | Ḍ– Ḍ Ṇ S R– Ṇ S , ‖
na – – – – – Je – – si – – – na – –

S M G M– R S Ṇ S R G M P , P– R , , G M P |
– ro – – – – – – Ye – – – – – mo – – – – –

R G M P D M , ,– D P M G M– R G, R– S R S |
Ne – – – – ne – – tlā – – – Tel – – – pu – –

N S Ḍ P̣ Ṃ Ḍ ,– Ḍ | Ṇ S R , , G M P ‖
du – – – – nam – – – – – – – ma – –

Anupallavi

D P M M   G G R S   D , N D   P , , ,–   P M D P |

– – – –   – – – –   Jā – Va –   – – – –   ra – – –

N D P M   G M R ,   G M P– R   P M G M   R G R S |

li – – –   ro – – –   Vi – – na   – – – –   – – – –

Ṇ S R S   , R– G M | P M , D   P M G M ‖

Ve – – –   – Sri – –   – – – –   – – – –

R P , M–   D N Ṡ ,   N Ṡ Ṙ Ṙ   , Ṙ– Ṙ Ġ   Ṁ Ġ , Ṁ |

Se – – –   sha – –   Cha – – –   – – le –   – – – –

Ṙ Ġ Ṙ Ṡ–   N Ṡ Ṙ Ġ   Ṙ Ṡ – N ,   Ṡ D N D ,   P – P M |

ndru – –   dai – – –   – – – na   – – – –   – – Sri –

Ṡ Ṙ N Ṡ   , Ṡ– P , | R , , G   M P– N D ‖

Ven – – –   – – ka –   te – – swa   – – ru –

D P M– M   G G R S

ni – – ki   – – – –

Mukthayi Swaram

, , , ,–   , , , ,   R G M P   , M G M–   R , G R |

S , S– Ḍ   Ṇ S R S   Ṇ , , Ṇ S– Ḍ   Ṇ Ḍ   P̣ , P̣ Ṃ |

Ḍ , Ḍ– Ṇ   , S– Ḍ N | S , R– Ṇ S R   G P ‖

M G M– R   G M P ,   D P M G , M– R P   M P , M |

D , N Ṡ   Ṙ Ġ , Ṁ–   Ṙ , Ġ Ṙ   Ṡ– N , Ṡ   D N D P |

R G M P   , P– Ṙ , | Ṙ Ṙ , Ṙ N ,   D P ‖

M G , M–   R G R S   (Evaremi)

Charanam

, , , ,– , , , , P , P , N D D P M , , , I
Pa – lu – mā – – – – – – –

G , G ,– R , G M– P ,– R G M P M G M– R G R I
ru – – – Ne – – – pi – la – – – – Chi – na – –

S , , Ṇ S R G , I M R G M P ,– P D II
Ra – – de – – – mi – Se – tu – – – ne –

Chittai Swaras

1. P , , M , , G , , , M ,– R , , ,– G , R , I
S , , ,– , , Ḍ ,– Ṇ , S ,– R , S ,– Ṇ , , , I
, , S ,– Ḍ , Ṗ , I Ṃ , Ḍ ,– , , Ṇ , II
S , R ,– G , M , (Palumāru)

2. P , D M P M– G , M R , G R S– R G M P , P I
N Ṡ Ṙ Ġ , Ṁ– Ṙ Ġ Ṙ N , Ṡ D P M– D , D N Ṡ I
Ṙ Ṡ , R G M P M I , D N Ṡ Ṙ– Ṡ , N II
D P ,– G M R G M (Palumāru)

3. N D D P M– G P N– G M R G M– P M G– M R G R I
S– Ṇ R Ṇ– S Ḍ Ṇ Ḍ R– S R Ṇ– S R G M P– R P M I
D N Ṡ– Ṙ Ġ Ṁ Ṙ Ġ I Ṙ– Ṡ Ṙ N Ṡ D– P D II
M– P M– G M R G M (Palumāru)

4. Ṡ , , Ṡ , Ṡ N Ṡ Ṙ– N , Ṡ– D , N D P M G M I
R , , G , M– R G M P , D– M P M G M– R G R I
S , , ,– R Ṇ S Ḍ I Ṇ Ḍ Ṗ Ṃ– Ḍ Ṇ S R II
S R Ṇ S , S– R G M P , P– M D ,– N Ṡ D N D I

P , M–D , N Ṡ ,– Ṙ ĠṀĠ , Ṁ–ṘĠ Ṙ Ṡ , , |
N, D P M, DN | Ṡ ṘṠ, Ṡ P ,– N ||
DPM–G MR GM (Palumāru)

6. YĒMISĒTUNE

Ragam	: BHAIRAVI — 20th Nata Bhairavi Janyam
Talam	: Khandajati Ata Talam
Arohanam	: S R_2 G_2 M_1 P D_1 N_2 Ṡ
Avarohanam	: Ṡ N_2 D_1 P M_1 G_2 R_2 S
Pallavi	: Yemisetune Ō Cheliyaro Ilaati Chelimi Jēsitini Gada
Anupallavi	: Bhaamaro Sri Venkateswarudaina Pantamulaadinatlu Saadhinchenu Gadā
Charanam	: Vadaredi Meragaadani Jūchu Chunnaanu ||

6. एमिसेतुने

राग : भैरवि
तालम् : खंडजाति अट तालम्

पल्लवि

एमिसेतुने ओ चेलियरो
इलाटि चेलिमि जेसितिनि गादा।।

अनुपल्लवि

भामरो श्रीवेंकटेश्वरूडैन
पंतमुलाडिनटुलु साधिंचेनु गदा।।

चरणं

वदरेदि मेर गादनि जूचुचुन्नानु।।

Pallavi 14×4 = 56

, , , , , , , , R , G , M R G , R , , , |
Ye – – – – – – – mi – – –

Ṇ S M G R S R G R S Ṇ Ḍ– Ṇ S R Ṇ Ḍ P̣ , Ḍ |
se – – – – tu – – – – – – ne – – – – Ō – –

Ṃ P̣ Ḍ Ṇ S , , Ḍ | Ṇ S R Ṇ S R G M ||
– – – – – – – che – – – li – – – ya

P D P P M G R S R G M G M R G S R G M Ṇ |
ro – – – – – – – I – – – – lā – – – – – ti

S R G M P D M P G R G M P D M , P D N Ṡ |
Che – – – li – mi – – – – – je – – – – – – –

P , D N Ṡ Ṙ N , | Ṡ P , D N Ṡ Ṙ Ṡ ||
si – – – – – – – ti ni – – – – – Ga

N D P M G G R S
– – – – dā – – –

Anupallavi

, , , ,– , , , , N N D D P–P M D D P P M |
Bhā – – – – – – ma – – –

M G M–P M G M R G S R G M G , R G M P M |
ro – – – – – – Sri – Ven – – – – ka – – – –

, P D M , P G R | G M– S R G M P D ||
– te – – – – – – swa – ru – – – – dai

M P D N Ṡ , , , N Ṡ P D P D N Ṡ Ṙ N , Ṡ |
na – – – – – – – Pan – – – – tha – – – – –

Ṙ ĠṀĠ ĠṘĠĠ Ṙ , NṠ ṘĠṠṘ NDNṠ ।
mu – – – – – la – – – di – – na – – tlu – –

ṘṠ , N DPDM । , GRG MPDN ॥
Sā – – – – dhi – – nche – – – – –

ṠP , D MGRS
– nu – ga – – dā –

Mukthayi Swaram

, , , , , , , , RGMG , RSR ṆSRG ।
MGRS RṆRṆ S , ṆR SṆḌṆ SP̣ , , ।
ḌṆSṆ , ṆSR । GM, R GMPD ॥
MPMG RSRG MPDP MGRG MPDN ।
ṠP , D NṠṘĠ , ṀĠṘ ṠṘND PMPD ।
NṠṘṠ , RG, । MPDP , ṘṠN ॥
DPMG RSṆS (Yemisetune)

Charanam

, , , ,– , , , , P , D , P , M – GRGM ।
Va – da – re – – – – – – –

P , , , P , , , MPDD PMGM PPMG ।
di – – – – – – – Me – – – ra – gā – – – – –

R GMR GSRS । R GMP D NṠṠ ॥
da – – ni – Jū – Chu Chu – – – nnā – – nu

Chittai Swaras

1. N , , ,   , , D ,   , , P ,   M , P ,   G , M , |
P , , ,   , , D ,   P , M ,   G , , R   , , S , |
N , , D   , , N , | S , R ,   , , G , ||
R , , G   , , M ,   (Vadarēdi)

2. M , P G   M R G ,   M R G S   R , G S   R Ṇ S , |
Ṇ S , Ṇ   R S Ṇ Ḍ   Ṇ S Ṗ Ḍ   , Ṗ Ḍ Ṇ   , S R S |
Ṇ R , R   G G , G | M M , M   P P , D ||
M P G R–   S R G M   (Vadarēdi)

3. N N D D   P M D D   P P M G   M P D M   P G M P |
R G M P   M P G R   G M G R   S Ṇ S R   G M P D |
N Ṡ Ṙ N   Ġ Ṙ N Ṙ | Ṡ Ṙ N D   P N D M ||
P M G R–   S R G M   (Vadarēdi)

4. Ṡ , , Ṡ   , Ṡ N Ṡ   Ṙ N , Ṙ   Ṡ N D P   M G R G |
M , P ,   N D P D   M P G M   P G , R   S R Ṇ , |
S , , Ṇ   G R Ṇ R | S R G M   P D , N ||
P D M P   G R G M   P N D M   P D N Ṡ   Ṙ Ġ Ṁ Ġ |
, Ṙ Ġ Ṡ   Ṙ N , D   P D N Ṡ   Ġ Ṙ Ġ Ṡ   , Ṙ N , |
Ṡ P , D   N Ṡ Ṙ Ṡ | , N D P   D M , G ||
R S Ṇ S   , R G M   (Vadaredi)

7. INKACHALAMĒLANAYYA

Ragam : CHAKRAVAKAM – 16th Melakarta Ragam
Talam : Khandajati Ata Talam
Arohanam : S R_1 G_3 M_1 P D_1 N_2 Ṡ
Avarohanam : Ṡ N_2 D_1 P M_1 G_3 R_1 S

Pallavi	: Inka Chalamelanayya Nāpai Idi mēra Kādura
Anupallavi	: Pankajāsanādi Vinutudaina Sri Venkateswara Samayamidera
Charanam	: Palumāru Ninne Nammiyunna Nannu Paalinchavayya

7. इंक चलमेलनय्या

राग : चक्रवाकम

तालम् : खंडजाति अट तालम्

पल्लवि

इंक चलमेलनय्या नापै
इदि मेर कादुरा

अनुपल्लवि

पंकजासनादि विनुतुडैन
श्री वेंकटेश्वर समयमिदेरा।।

चरणं

पलुमारू निन्ने नम्मियुन्न
नन्नु पालिन्चवय्या।।

Pallavi 14×4 = 56

, , , ,   , , , ,   G , M ,   R , , ,–   S Ṇ Ḍ Ṇ ।
In – – –   Ka – – –   Cha – – –

S , , ,–   S , , ,–   Ṇ S R R   S Ṇ– Ḍ Ṇ   S S Ṇ Ḍ ।
la – – –   – – – –   me – – –   – – la –   – – – –

P̣ Ḍ Ṇ S   , R– Ṇ S । R G ,– M   P M– G M ॥

na – – –   – – yya   – – – na   – –   – –

G R S– Ṇ   Ḍ Ṇ S R   G M G G   R R S S   , Ṇ Ḍ Ṇ |
pai – – –   – – – –   Idi – –   – – – –   – – – –

S R G M   ,– P M G–   M D P D   , M G R–   P M G R |
me – – –   – – – –   ra – – –   – – – –   Kā – – – |

S , , Ṇ   – Ḍ Ṇ S, | , Ṡ   N Ṙ–   Ṡ , N D ||
– – – –   – – – – –   – du – –   – – – –

Anupallavi

P M G R   S– Ṇ S R   Ṡ N D D   P M– P D   P P M G |
ra – – –   – – – –   Pan – –   – – Ka –   – – – –

M D P D   , D– R S   M G , M–   P M G R–   S Ṇ Ḍ Ṇ |
ja – – –   – – sa –   na – – –   di – – –   Vi – – –

S S R– S   , R– M G | M P , M–   G M P D ||
nu – – –   – – tu –   – – – –   dai – – –

M P D N   Ṡ , , ,   N D P D   , D– N Ṡ   Ṙ N , Ṡ |
na – – –   – – – –   Sri – –   – – Ven –   – – – –

Ġ Ṙ Ġ Ġ   , Ṁ Ġ Ṙ–   Ṡ Ġ Ṙ Ṙ   Ṡ N– D Ṡ   N N D P |
ka – – –   – – – –   te – – –   – – swa   ra – – –

M D P P   M G– M P | D N Ṡ Ṙ   Ṡ , N D ||
Sa – ma –   – – – –   ya – – –   mi – – –

P M G R   S– Ṇ S R
de – – –   – ra – –

Mukthayi Swaram

, , , ,– , , , , G , M G R S R , G R S Ṇ |

S R Ṇ S– Ṇ Ḍ P̣ Ṃ– P̣ Ḍ Ṇ S , S– Ḍ Ṇ S R , R |

G S R G , G– M P | D P , M G R S Ṇ ||

S R G M P , , , M G R S , R– G M P D , N |

Ṡ Ṙ Ġ Ṁ Ġ , Ṙ Ṡ– N D N Ṡ N , D P M– G M P |

D N Ṡ– R G M P D | N– Ṡ Ṙ Ṡ , N D P ||

M G R S ,– Ṇ S R (Inka Chalamela)

Charanam

, , , ,– , , , , P , M , P , , ,– P M G M |
Pa – lu – ma – – – ru – – –

P D N D– P , D P M G M ,– P M G R– S Ṇ Ḍ N |
Ni – – – nne – Na – – mmi – yu – – – nna – –

S R G M ,– P M G | M P D N Ṡ , N D ||
Na – nnu – – Pa – – lin – ncha - – – Vayya

Chittai Swaras

1. P , ,– M , ,– G , , ,– R , S , Ṇ ,– Ḍ , N , |
S , , ,– , ,– R , S , Ṇ , Ḍ , P̣ , M , , , |
, , P̣ ,– Ḍ ,– Ṇ , | S , R ,– S , , , ||
, , R ,– G , M , (Palumāru)

2. P D N D , P– M P D P , M G R S Ṇ– Ḍ Ṇ S R |
G M G R , S– N D P M , G– R G– S R G M P D |
N Ṡ Ṙ– Ṡ , N D P | D P , M G R S Ṇ ||
S Ḍ , Ṇ– S R G M (Palumāru)

3. P D N N D P – M P D D P M – G M R G M P D N |
S R G M P D N Ṡ – Ṙ Ṡ N D N Ṡ – Ġ Ṙ Ġ Ṁ Ġ Ṙ |
Ṡ Ṙ Ṡ N D P – N D | P M G – D P M G R ||
S Ṇ Ḍ – Ṇ S R G M (Palumāru)

4. Ṡ , , Ṙ Ṡ N – D N Ṡ Ṡ N D – P D N N D P – M G |
M P D N , Ṡ – G M P D , N – D P M G R S Ṇ Ḍ |
Ṇ S R G , M S , | R – G , M P , D N ||
Ṡ Ṙ Ṡ N , D – N Ṡ Ṙ Ġ , Ṁ – Ṡ Ṙ Ġ Ṁ Ġ Ġ Ṙ Ṡ |
D N Ṡ Ṙ – Ṡ Ṡ N D – P G , M P D N Ṡ , Ṡ – G M |
P D , D N Ṡ Ṙ Ġ | Ṁ Ġ Ṙ – Ṡ , N D P ||
M G R S , – R G M (Palumāru)

PADA VARNAM

8. SĀMI NINNĒ

Ragam : ATANA — 29th Dheera Sankarabharanam Janyam

Talam : Khandajati Ata Talam

Arohanam : S R_2 M_1 P N_3 Ṡ

Avarohanam : Ṡ N_3 D_2, P M_1 G_3 M_1 R_2 S

Pallavi : Sāmi ninnē kōriyunnadirā Mā
Sārasākshi neekaina chinnadirā

Anupallavi : Sreeman mahā mēru samāna dheerudaina
Sree ugra pāndya bhūpāla gānalōla

Mukthāyi Swara
Sāhithyam : Nee Nerathanamunakā
cheli thāthakunu dāni sugunamulanu
ne pogada — jālanu sadāmadini ninnu
dalachi chāla thamimeeri ninnu thodi

themmanenurā — parākujēya thagadurā
nijamu palkithinirā ika birāna rā rā
Dheerā! sukumārā nara vara

Charanam : Nee Rākakeduru Jūchu chunnadira

Chittai Swara Sāhithyās :

1. Neevē gāna yōgasālivi neevē rasika
   Sikhāmani yani chālavini (Nee)
2. Ata pāta palu needu kulukumari jūdu
   palukulaku mēdimikala ala
   bōdika nimishavathudu lella sari sātiyu
   kārani nādi palkuthunu (Nee)
3. Karakara madiya kumāruni saramula
   kedari bedari badari virahamunu
   thapana kiranamu kalasi tharuni ninu dalachi
   Tharunamidi Ikanu chiramu Tha Gādanuchu (Nee)
4. Pāpāthmudagu māruni bōdhanaku lōbadi
   vacchina — Malaya māruthudu
   thanakāpthudou yanaru nee gunamunu
   chēkonanu sukakaramulaina
   mrigamadādi sumasugandamul
   hithavu — lēdanuchunu Saiyyapai poruluchu
   sārekunu ninnu madilō thalachuchununna
   cheli (Nee)

8. सामि निन्ने (पद वर्णम)

राग : अठाना
तालम् : खंडजाति अट तालम्

पल्लवि

सामि निन्ने कोरि युन्नदिरा
सारसाक्षि नीकैन चिन्नदिरा

अनुपल्लवि

श्रीमन महा मेरु समान धीरुडैन
श्री उग्र पाण्डय भूपाल गानलोल

मुक्ताई स्वर साहिम्यम

नी नेरतनमुनका
चेलि तातकुनु दानि सुगुणमुलनु
ने पोगड जालनु सदामदिनि निन्नु
दलचि चाल तमिमीरि निन्नु तोडि
तेम्मनेनुरा पराकुजेय तगदुरा
निजमु पलिकितिनिरा इक बिरान रारा
धीरा सुकुमार नर वर ॥ (सामि निन्ने)

चरणं

नी राककेदुरु जूचु चुन्नदिरा ॥

चिट्टैस्वर साहित्य

1. नीवे गान योगिशालिवि नीवे रसिक
   सिखामणि यनि चालविनि (नी राककेदुरु)

2. आट पाट पलु नीदु कुलुकुमार जूडु
   पलुकुलकु मेलिमिकल अल
   बोडिक निमिषवतुडु लेल्ल सरि साटियु
   कारनि नादि पलुकुदुनु ॥ (नी राककेदुरु)

3. करकर मदिय कुमारुनि सरमुल
   केदरि बेदरि बदरि विरहमुनु
   तपन किरनमु कलसि तरूनि निनु दलचि
   तरूणमिदि इकनु चिरमु ता गादनुचु ॥ (नी राककेदुरु)

4. पापात्मुडगु मारुनि बोधनकु लोबडि
   वच्चिन-मलय मारुतुडु

तनकाप्तुडै यनरु नी गुणमुनु
चेकोननु सुखकरमुलैन
मृगमदादि सुमसुगंधदमुल
हितवु लेदनुचुनु सैय्यपै पोरलुचु
सारेकुनु निन्नु मदिलो तलचुचुनुन्न चेलि।। (नी राककेदुरु)

Pallavi 14×4 =56

, , , , , , , , * Ṡ , , , Ṡ N P , D , D , ।
– – – – – – – – Sā – – – – – – – mi – – –

P D P Ṡ Ṡ N P , D D P , M D P– M , P M G ।
ni – – – – – – – nnē – – kō – – – – – – –

G M P– D D P– P , । M– P Ṡ N Ṡ N D N ॥
ri – – – – – yu – – nna – – – di –

Ṡ ,– Ṡ D P M P N * Ṡ Ṙ N Ṡ N P– D D P M– P Ṡ ।
– – ra – – mā – – sā – – – – – ra – – – sā –

D , ,– P M D P , ,– M R M R , S– Ṇ , S R S ।
– – – kshi – – – – – nee – – – – – kai – – – –

M M R– P P M– D D । P– Ṡ N Ṙ Ṡ N– D , ॥
na – – – – – chi – – nna – – – – di –

Anupallavi

P M P– G , M P N * P , , , P D P P M G– M P ।
– – – ra – – – – Sree – – man – – – – – ma –

M , ,– G M P D P D , ,– P D M P , M– P Ṡ N ।
hā – – mē – – ru – sa – – mā – – – – – na – –

D , P– M   , P– G M | R , S– Ṇ   S R M R ||
– – – dhee   – – ru –   – – – dai   – – – –

M P Ṡ N   Ṡ , , , * P   N Ṡ Ṙ   , Ṡ– N Ṡ   D , N Ṡ |
– – – –   na – – –   Sree – – –   – – U –   gra – – –

Ṁ Ġ Ṁ Ṙ   , Ṡ– N Ṡ   Ṙ– N , Ṡ   Ṡ   D P M   R M P N |
pā – – –   – – ndya   – – – –   Bhū – – –   pā – – –

Ṡ Ṙ N Ṡ   N P– D D | P M R– G   M R S , ||
la – – –   – – gā –   – – – na   – – lō –

,– M R P   M– N P R *
– la – –   – – – –

Mukthāyi Swara Sāhithyam

, , , ,   , , , , * Ṡ   , N P   D P M P   G , M P |
– – – –   – – – –   Nee – ne ra   tha na mu na   kā – che li

D , ,– P   Ṡ N D ,   ,– P D N   Ṡ Ṙ Ṡ N   D , P M |
tha – – tha   ku nu dā –   – ni su gu   na mu la nu   nē – po ga

P– Ṡ , Ṡ   N Ṡ D , | P   M P– G   ,– M R S ||
da jā – la   nu sa dā –   ma di ni nin   – nu da la

R– Ṇ , S R M P   , * P– N Ṡ Ṙ   , Ṡ– G ,   M P M– D |
chi Chā – la tha mi mee –   ri ni nu thō   – di them ma ne nu rā

,– P Ṡ ,   N– Ṙ , Ṡ   Ġ Ṁ Ṙ Ṡ   ,– Ṙ N Ṡ   D , N Ṡ |
– pa rā –   ku je – ya   tha ga du rā   – ni ja mu   pal – ki thi

Ṙ Ṡ ,– Ṡ N P– D , I Ṗ– Ṡ , Ṡ P , M– G ‖
ni rā – I ka bi rā – na rā – ra Dhee – ra Su

M R , S R M P N *
ku ma – ra na ra va ra (Sāmi)

Charanam

, , , , , , , , * N , Ṡ , Ṡ N N D N , Ṡ , I
– – – – – – – – Nee – – – – – – – rā – – –

M P N Ṡ R Ṡ N P D D P , M P Ṡ D , P– M D I
ka – – – ne – du – ru – – – jū – – – , – chu –

P M , P M G– G M I P– D , P Ṡ N Ṡ , ‖
Chu – – – – – nna – – – – di – – ra –

Chittai Swara Sāhihyās

1. P , , , Ṡ , , , N , Ṡ , D , , , N , Ṡ , I
Nee – – – vē – – – gā – na – yō – – – ga – sā –

, ,– N , Ṙ , Ṡ , , ,– P , , ,– Ṡ , N , P , I
– – li – vi – nee – – – vē – – – ra – si – ka –

M , G , , ,– M , I R , S , R , S , ‖
si – kā – – – ma – ni – ya – ni – Chā –

, ,– R , M , P , *
– – la – vi – ni – (Nee)

2. Ṡ , N D ,– P M P D , P– M P M G M R , M P I
Ā – ta pā – ta pa lu nee – du ku lu ku ma ri jū – du pa

D P– Ṡ N D , P– M P Ṡ N Ṡ Ġ , Ṙ Ṡ N Ṡ Ṙ Ṡ |

lu ku la ku mē – li mi ka la a la bō – di ka ni mi sha va

N , Ṡ– D , N Ṡ Ṙ | Ṡ , N P D , P M ||

thu – du lel – la sa ri sā – ti yu gā – ra ni

G , R– S , R M P *

nā – di pal – Ku thu nu (Nee)

3. P N P– M P– G M P D P M– G M R S– Ṇ S R– S M |

Ka ra ka ra ma di ya ku mā ru ni sa ra mu la ke da ri be da

R– M P M D D P– M P Ṡ N Ṡ P N Ṡ Ṙ Ṡ– Ṁ Ġ Ṁ |

ri ba da ri vi ra ha mu nu tha pa na ki ra na mu – ka la si

Ṙ Ṡ Ṙ– Ṡ N D N Ṡ | Ṙ Ṡ N P D– M P M ||

tha ru ni ni nu da la chi tha ru na mi di i ka nu

G M R– R S R M P *

chi ra mu thā gā da nu chu (Nee)

4. P , ,– P , M D P– M D P– M , P– M P G , M P |

Pā – – pā – thm uda gu mā ru ni bō – da na ku lō – ba di

D , , , P D P Ṡ N D , P M D P M P , , , |

va – – – cchi na ma la ya mā – ru thu du tha na kā – – –

Ṙ Ṡ ,– N Ṡ N– P D | P M P– G , M R S ||

pthudou ya na ru nee gu na mu nu chē – ko na nu

Ṇ S R M P D , D M P N Ṡ , Ṡ– N Ṡ Ṙ N , Ṡ |

Su kha ka ra mu lai – na mri ga ma dā – di su ma su gan – da

D , NṠ ṀĠ, Ṁ ṘṠ Ṙ–N , ṠD , P MPN |
mul– hitha vu lē– da nu chu nu sai – yi pai– po ra lu chu

Ṡ , ,– Ṡ N P D , | ,– P M P G , ,– M ||
Sā – – re kụ nu nin – – nu ma di lō – – da

R Ṇ S , ,– R M P *
la chu chun – – na che li (Nee)

❋❋❋

9

Kritis of Patnam Subramanya Iyer

(Lyrics Only)

1. NEEVEGATIYANI

Ragam : PURNACHANDRIKA –
29th Dheera Sankarabharanam Janyam

Talam : ADI

Arohanam : S R_2 G_3 M_1 P D_2 P $\dot{S}$

Avarohanam : $\dot{S}$ N_3 P M_1 R_2 G_3 M_1 R_2 S

Pallavi : Neeve Gatiyani Chāla Nammi
Nee Sannidhikori Vachchinānayya

Anupallavi : Kāveri Teera Vāsollāsa Jagadheesa
Kāmita Dāyaka Sri Panchanadheesa
Sarvesa

Charanam : Dharalo Ninnu Nammina vāralake
Bhāgyamu Kalgunanuchu Sthiramuga
Sri Venkateswarudu Balkinadi Telusukontini
Karunākara Pāmara janula Sēva chēsi
Chāla veda Jenditini Nā Paritāpamulella
Deerchi Brova Samayamide Pranathārthi
Hara

1. नीवेगतियनि

राग : पूर्णचन्द्रिका
तालम् : आदि

पल्लवि

नीवेगतियनि चाला नम्मि
नी सन्निधि कोरि वच्चिनानय्या।।

अनुपल्लवि

कावेरि तीर वासोल्लास जगधीश
कामित दायक श्री पंचनधीश सर्वेश।। (नीवेगति)

चरणं

धरलो निन्नु नम्मिन वारलके
भाग्यमु कलगुननुचु स्थिरमुगा
श्री वेंकटेश्वरुडु बलिकिनदि तेलुसुकोंटिनि
करुणाकर पामर जनुल सेव चेसि
चाला वेद जेन्दितिनि ना परितापमुलेल्ल दीर्चि
ब्रोव समयमिदे प्रणतार्थि हर (नीवेगतिथनि)

2. NĀYEDA NEEKABHIMĀNAMU

Ragam	: BEGADA — 29th Dheera Sankarabharanam Janyam
Talam	: MISRA CHĀPU
Arohanam	: S R_2 G_3 M_1 P D_2 P $\dot{S}$
Avarohanam	: $\dot{S}$ N_3 D_2 P M_1 G_3 R_2 S
Pallavi	: Nāyeda Neekabhimānamu Ledāyane Sri Ramā
Anupallavi	: Toyajaptākula Tilaka Ne Tolijēsina Pujāphalamemo

Charanam : Nādu Sankatamulanu Neeto Nānātiki
Delpaga Ledā
Ādaramugā Nannu Veravakumanarāda
Nātonu vāda
Sri Venkateswara Nāchintala Deerpa rāda

2. नायेड नीकभिमानमु

राग : बेगड
तालम् : मिश्रचापु

पल्लवि

नायेड नीकभिमानमु लेदायने श्रीरामा।।

अनुपल्लवि

तोयजाप्तकुल तिलक ने तोलिजेसिन पूजाफलमेमो।। (नायेड)

चरणं

नादु संकटमुलनु नीतो नानाटिकि तेल्पग लेदा।
आदरमुग नन्नु वेरवकुमनरादा नातोनु वादा।
श्रीवेंकटेश्वर ना चिन्तल दीर्परादा। (नायेड)

3. EVARUNNARU

Ragam : SIMHAVAHINI – 27th Sarasangi Janyam
Talam : ADI
Arohanam : S G_3 M_1 P D_1 N_3 $\dot{S}$
Avarohanam : $\dot{S}$ N_3 D_1 P M_1 G_3 R_2 S
Pallavi : Evarunnāru Nannu Brōchutaku
Inavamsa vara kumāra Dheera
Anupallavi : Bhuvanāsraya Mohana Sri Ramana
Bhūbhāra Harana Bhudhavarēnya
Charanam : Sakalēswara Sādhu hrit Sanchāra
Sakala Durjana Samhāra Sūra
Sakalāgama Sannuta charitra
Sakalābheeshtaja yoga Sri Venkatesa

3. एवरून्नारू

राग : सिंहवाहिनी
तालम् : आदि

पल्लवि

एवरून्नारू ननु ब्रोचुटकू
इनवंश वर कूमार धीर

अनुपल्लवि

भुवनश्रय मोहन श्री रमण
भूभार हरण बुधवरेण्य।। (एवरुन्नारु)

चरणं

सकलेश्वर साधु ह्रित संचार
सकल दुर्जन संहार शूर
सकलागम सन्नुत चरित्र
सकलाभीष्टज योग श्री वेंकटेश (एवरून्नारू)

4. VERUVANELA

Ragam	: SUDDHA BANGALA — 22nd Kharaharapriya Janyam
Talam	: RUPAKAM
Arohanam	: S R_2 M_1 P D_2 $\dot{S}$
Avarohanam	: $\dot{S}$ D_2 P M_1 R_2 G_2 R_2 S
Pallavi	: Veruvanela Ō Manasa Vēmāru Ne delpa Lēda
Anupallavi	: Marimari Nē Nēmoyenchi Mātimātiki Itula Neevu
Charanam	: Parama Dukkha karamula I Bhavapāsamulona Tagili Verachuchunu Charanamulaina Narulato Brochina Ne Sthiramugānu Nammina

Sri Bhogasayanudaina
Varada Venkateswarudu Nirvahinchedadani
Telisiyundaga

4. वेरुवनेल

राग : शुद्बंगाल
तालम् : रूपकं

पल्लवि

वेरुवनेल वो मनसा वेमारू ने देल्प लेदा।

अनुपल्लवि

मरिमरि ने नेमोएंचि माटिमाटिकि इटुल नीवु।। (वेरूवनेल)

चरणं

परम दुख़ करमुल ई भवपाशमुलोन तगिलि।
वेरचुचुनु चरणमुलैन नरूलतो ब्रोचिन।
ने स्थिरमुगानु नम्मिन श्री भोगशयनुडैन।
वरद वेंकटेश्वरूडु निर्वहिंचेदडनि तेलिसियुंडग।। (वेरूवनेल)

5. MARACHĒDI NYAYAMA

Ragam : HAMSADHWANI –
29th Dheera Sankarabharana Janyam
Talam : ADI
Arohanam : $S\ R_2\ G_3\ P\ N_3\ \dot{S}$
Avarohanam : $\dot{S}\ N_3\ P\ G_3\ R_2\ S$
Pallavi : Marachēdi Nyāyama Rāmā Neeve
Marachite Vēre gati evarayya
Anupallavi : Sarasiruhāsana Pujitāmsa Charana
Sanātana Dheenulanu
Charanam : Kali Rāja Kinkarula Atikraminchi
Kanalēni Himsala Jēyuchunde
Khala Samhārudane Keerti Neeku Kaligenu
Phalamu Sri Venkatesa

5. मरचेदि न्यायमा

राग : हंसध्वनि

तालम् : आदि

पल्लवि

मरचेदि न्यायमा रामा
नीवे मरचिते वेरे गति एवरय्या।।

अनुपल्लवि

सरसीरुहासन पूजितांस चरण
सनातन धीनुलनु।। (मरचेदि)

चरणं

कलि राज किंकरुल अतिक्रमिंचि
कनलेनि हिंसल जेयुचुन्डे
खल संहरुडने कीर्ति नीकू
कलिगेनु फलमु श्री वेंकटेश।। (मरचेदि)

6. MARIVEREDIKKAVVARO

Ragam	: LATANGI— 63rd Melakarta Ragam
Talam	: KHANDA JHAMPE
Arohanam	: S R_2 G_3 M_2 P D_1 N_3 $\dot{S}$
Avarohanam	: $\dot{S}$ N_3 D_1 P M_2 G_3 R_2 S
Pallavi	: Marivere Dikkevvaro Rāmayya
Anupallavi	: Dharalona Nee Sāti Daivamevvaruleka
Charanam	: Manasāra Ninu Sāramagu Sankeertanamu Onarincha Vinavēmi Varada Venkateswara

6. मरि वेरे दिक्केव्वरो

राग : लतांगि
तालम् : आदि

पल्लवि

मरिवेरे दिक्केव्वरो रामय्या।।

अनुपल्लवि

धरलोन नी साटि दैवमेव्वरु लेक।। (मरि वेरे दिक्केव्वरो)

चरणं

मनसार निनु सारमगु संकीर्तनमु
ओनरिंच विनवेमि वरद वेंकटेश्वरा।। (मरि वेरे दिक्केव्वरो)

7. ENNADU NEEKRIPA

Ragam : VĀCHASPATI – 64th Melakarta Ragam
Talam : ADI
Arohanam : S R_2 G_3 M_2 P D_2 N_2 $\dot{S}$
Avarohanam : $\dot{S}$ N_2 D_2 P M_2 G_3 R_2 S
Pallavi : Ennadu Neekripa Kalguno
Inakula Tilaka Nanu Rakshinchutaku
Anupallavi : Pannaga Sayana Patita Pāvana
Bhānukula Deepa Bhavanāsachāpa
Charanam : Kanna Tandri Nāpai Karuninchamani
Kannavāri Ninne Āsrayinchitini
Ninnu Nera Nammi yunna vādani neeto
Vinnavinchukonti Venkatesa Nāpai

7. एन्नडु नीकृप

राग : वाचस्पति
तालम् : आदि

पल्लवि

एन्नडु नीकृप कलगुनो
इनकुल तिलक ननु रक्षिंचुटकु

अनुपल्लवि

पन्नग शयन पतित पावन
भानुकुल दीप भवनाशचाप (एन्नडु)

चरणं

कन्न तन्ड्रि नापै करुणिंचमनि
कन्नवारि निन्ने आश्रयिंचितिनि
निन्नु नेर नम्मि युन्नवाडनि नीतो
विन्नविंचुकोन्टि वेंकटेश नापै (एन्नडु)

8. SREEKARA RAGHUVEERA

Ragam	: SĀRASWATI – 64th Vāchaspati Janyam
Talam	: RUPAKAM
Arohanam	: S R_2 M_2 P D_2 Ṡ
Avarohanam	: Ṡ N_2 D_2 P M_2 R_2 S
Pallavi	: Srikara Raghuveera Sritajana Mandāra
Anupallavi	: Lokāteeta Sukhyāta Lokādhāra Dheera
Charanam	: Naravara Kamalādhara Natajana Dhuritāpahara Karunākara Venkatesa Khala Samhāra

8. श्रीकर रघुवीर

राग : सरस्वति
तालम् : रूपकं

पल्लवि

श्रीकर रघुवीर श्रितजन मन्दार।।

अनुपल्लवि

लोकातीत सुख्यात लोकाधार धीर।। (श्रीकर रघुवीर)

चरणं

नरवर कमलाधार नतजन
धुरिताप हर करूणाकर वेंकटेश खल संहार (श्रीकर रघुवीर)

9. PANCHANADHEESA PĀHIMAM

Ragam : PURNACHANDRIKA –
29th Dheera Sankarabharana Janyam
Talam : RUPAKAM
Arohanam : S R_2 G_3 M_1 P D_2 P $\dot{S}$
Avarohanam : $\dot{S}$ N_3 P M_1 R_2 G_3 M_1 R_2 S
Pallavi : Panchanadheesa Pāhimam Bhavadheesa Sarvesa
Anupallavi : Sanchita karma Samana chara chara pālana Dhureena
Charanam 1) Darukavana vihāra Dakshadhwarahara Chatura
Veerabhadrajanaka Venkatesa Mōdakara
2) Soora Samhāra Kumārajanaka Pranavārtha Swaroopa
Srikāntha mudita Hridayāravinda Sadānanda

9. पंचनधीश पाहिमां

राग : पूर्णचन्द्रिक
तालम् : रूपकं

पल्लवि

पंचनधीश पाहिमां
भवाधीश सर्वेश

अनुपल्लवि

संचित कर्म शमन चरा–
–चर पालन धुरीन।। (पंचनधीश)

चरणं

1. दरुकवन विहार दक्षाध्वरहर चतुर।
वीरभद्रजनक वेंकटेश मोदकर।। (पंचनधीश)
2. सूर संहार कूमारजनक प्रणवार्थ स्वरूप।
श्रीकांत मुदित हृदयानंद सदानंद।। (पंचनधीश)

10. PANCHAPAKESWARENA

Ragam	: RAMAPRIYA – 52nd Melakarta Ragam
Talam	: ADI
Arohanam	: S R_1 G_3 M_2 P D_2 N_2 $\dot{S}$
Avarohanam	: $\dot{S}$ N_2 D_2 P M_2 G_3 R_1 S
Pallavi	: Panchapākeswarena Paripālitoham Sada
Anupallavi	: Panchānanena Trymbakena Pranava Nādaswaroopena
Charanam	: Pancha Bānāpaghana Dahanena Pra- Pancha Srushti Sthithi Laya karanena Pancha charajanaka Venkatesahitena

Pancha bhootakarena Sarvena
Pancha Bhootātmakena Rudrena
Pancha Bhootāteetena Bhavena
Panchākshara Sadanena Sivena

10. पंचपाकेश्वरेण

राग : रामप्रिय
तालम् : आदि

पल्लवि

पंचपाकेश्वरेण परिपालितोहम सदा।

अनुपल्लवि

पंचाननेन त्रयंबकेन प्रणव नादश्वरूपेण।। (पंचपाकेश्वरेण)

चरणं

पंच बाणापघन धहनेन प्रपंच
श्रृष्टि स्थिति लय करनेण
पंच प्राणाधार भूतेण
पंच चरजनक वेंकटेशहितेन
पंच भूतकरेण सर्वेण
पंच भूतात्मकेन रूद्रेण
पंच भूतातीतेन भवेन
पचांक्षर सदानेन शिवेन।। (पंचपाकेश्नरेण)

11. HAR HARA SMARAHARA

Ragam : MANGALAKAISIKI – 15th Mayamalava Goula Janyam
Talam : ADI
Arohanam : S M_1 G_3 M_1 P D_1 N_3 $\dot{S}$
Avarohanam : $\dot{S}$ N_3 D_1 P M_1 G_3 R_1 S

Pallavi : Harahara Smarahara Girijāvara San-
Kara Gangādhara Tripurahara Mrigadhara

Anupallavi : Parama Dayākara Bhaktajana mandāra
Bhavabhayahara Sri panchanadeeswara

Charanam : Dandadharagarva Khanda Nāsana
Mārkanda Varada Vedanta Charmādhara
Andapinda Brahmānda Vyapaka Prachanda
Koti Mārthānda Nibhānga Dandita
Dakshakhandalādi Soora
Mandala Munijana shanda kamala
Mārthāndakaralādhara mandana vakra
Tundajanka Sri chandikā Ramana

11. हरहर स्मरहर

राग : मंगलकैशिक
तालम् : आदि

पल्लवि

हरहर स्मरहर गिरिजावर शंकर
गंगाधर त्रिपुरहर मृगधर।।

अनुपल्लवि

परम दयाकर भक्तजन मन्दार
भवभयहर श्री पंचनदीश्वर।। (हरहर स्मरहर)

चरणं

दण्डधर गर्व खंडनाशन मर–
–कंड वरद वेदान्त चरमाधर
अंडपिंड भ्रहमांड व्यापक प्रचंड
कोटि मार्ताण्ड निभंग दण्डित
दक्क्षखंडलादि शूर

मण्डल मुनिजन शंड कमल
मार्ताण्डकरलाधर मंदन वक्र
तुंडजनक श्री चण्डिका रमण (हरहर स्मरहर)

Note: As mentioned by the author of the book "P.S. Iyer Apoorva Sāhityangal — Harikesanallur Veenai A. Subramanyam, the above Kriti was found among the other compositions of P.S. Iyer. So it has been considered as one of P.S. Iyer's composition.

12. SRIPANCHANADEESAM

Ragam : SAHĀNA — 28th Harikambhoji Janyam
Talam : RUPAKAM
Arohanam : S R_2 G_3 M_1 P M_1 D_2 N_2 $\dot{S}$
Avarohanam : $\dot{S}$ N_2 D_2 P M_1 G_3 M_1 R_2 G_3 R_2 S
Pallavi : Sri Panchanadeesam Chintāyamyaham
Anisam
Anupallavi : Tāpatrayānalavarunam Darukavana
Viharanam
Pāpatuhina Ravikiranam Parātparam
Bhavataranam
Charanam : Sarvābheeshta pradam Panchanada
Kshetradharam
Sarveswaram Sri Dharmasamvardhanee
Manoharam
Sarva Mangalakaram Jagatgurum
Maheswaram
Sarvārishtādi Vimochanakaram
Jalpeswaram
Sarvajeeva Dayākaram Chaturdasa
Bhuvaneswaram
Sarvopanishat sāram Sannuta
Venkateswaram

12. श्रीपंचनदीशम

राग : शहन
तालम् : रूपकं

पल्लवि

श्रीपंचनदीशम चिन्तयाम्यहम अनिशम।।

अनुपल्लवि

तापत्रयानलवरूणम दरुकवन विहरनं
पापतुहिन रविकिरनं परात्परम भवतरणम।। (श्रीपंचनदीशम)

चरणं

सर्वाभीष्टप्रदम पंचनद क्षेत्रधरं
सर्वेश्वरम श्रीधर्मसंवर्धनी मनोहरं
सर्वमंगलकरं जगतगुरुम महेश्वरं
सर्वश्रिष्टादि विमोचनकरं जलपेश्वरं
सर्वजीव दयाकरं चर्तदुश भुवनेश्वरं
सर्वोपनिषत शरं सन्नुत वेंकेश्वरं।। (श्रीपंचनदीशम)

13. BHAJARE MĀNASA

Ragam	: SUGUNABHOOSHANI — 22nd Kharaharapriya Janyam
Talam	: RUPAKAM
Arohanam	: S G_2 M_1 P M_1 D_2 N_2 Ṡ
Avarohanam	: Ṡ N_2 D_2 P M_1 D_2 M_1 R_2 S
Pallavi	: Bhajare Mānasa Sri Pranatārthiharam Sadā
Anupallavi	: Ajapidaujādi Vanditam Ādimadyāntha rahitam

Rajata Bhootarāsthitam Ravikoti Sankāsam
Tam

Charanam : Charācharātmakam Virāja Rājita Jatādharam
Parātparam Haram Chidambarādipam
Digambaram
Parāsaktivaram Bhakta parādeenam
Sankaram
Murāri Sri Venkateswararādhitam Iswaram
Nirāmayam Nirvikāram Niranjanam
Nirākāram
Nirālambam Nirādharam
Nirantarānandakaram

13. भजरेमानस

राग : सुगुणभूषणि
तालम् : रूपकं

पल्लवि

भजरे मानस श्री प्रणतार्थिहरं सदा।

अनुपल्लवि

अजपिडौजादि वन्दितं आदिमद्यात्म रहितं।
रजत भूतरस्थितं रविकोटि शंकाशं तं।। (भजरेमानस)

चरणं

चराचरात्मकं विराज राजित जटाधरमं।
परात्परं हरं चिदंबरादिपं दिगम्बरं।
पराशक्तिवरं भक्त परादीनं शंकरं।
मुरारि श्री वेंकटेश्वराधितं ईश्वरं।
निरामयं निर्विकारं निरंजनं निराकरं।
निरालम्बं निराधरं निरंतरानन्दकरं।। (भजरेमानस)

14. PĀLAYA SRI

Ragam	: SANKARABHARANAM – 29th Melakarta Ragam
Talam	: ADI
Arohanam	: S R_2 G_3 M_1 P D_2 N_3 $\dot{S}$
Avarohanam	: $\dot{S}$ N_3 D_2 P M_1 G_3 R_2 S
Pallavi	: Pālaya Sri Panchanadeeswaram Pālaya Dharmāmbika Manohara
Anupallavi	: Phala Netra Kamaneeya Gātra Parama Pavitra Sachcharitra
Charanam	: Tāpatrayānala Vārivāha Dāsajanārti Jaladha Gandharva Rūpavijitāyuta Madana Janaugha Moksha Dhatha Tripurāsura samhāra Sripati Venkateswarollasa Srikara Rajatādri Nivāsa Āhika Lābha Sudhākara Kalavadhamsa Lalita Bhāsha Poshitākhila Sumanasa

14. पालय श्री

राग : शंकराभरणं

तालम् : आदि

पल्लवि

पालय श्री पंचनदीश्वरं
पालय धर्माम्बिक मनोहर।।

अनुपल्लवि

फल नेत्र कमनीय गात्र
परम पवित्र सच्चरित्र।। (पालय श्री)

चरणं

तापत्रयानल वारिवाह।
दासजनार्ति जलध गन्धर्व।
रूपविजितायुत मदन जनौघ।
मोक्षदात त्रिपुरासुर संहार।
श्रीपति वेंकटेश्वरोल्लास।
श्रीकर रजताद्रि निवास आहिक।
लाभ सुधाकर कलवधंश।
ललित भाष पोषिताखिल सुमनस। (पालय श्री)

15. ETUNAMMINĀVO

Ragam : SĀVERI – 15th Mayamalava Goula Janyam
Talam : ADI
Arohanam : S R_1 M_1 P D_1 $\dot{S}$
Avarohanam : $\dot{S}$ N_3 D_1 P M_1 G_3 R_1 S
Pallavi : Etu Nammināvo Manasa Inchukaina
Bhodhana Cheyalēda
Anupallavi : Chedukanti Rōga Peeditamai Chedi
Ksheeninche Dēhamu Sthiramani
Charanam : Mattikunda Kante Heenamainadidi
Māti mātiki Rādu Deenipai
Vatti mohamu Jenduchunu
Varada Venkateswaruni Marachi

15. एटुनम्मिनावो

राग : सावेरि
तालम् : आदि

पल्लवि

एटुनम्मिनावो मनसा
इन्चुकैन भोधन चेयलेदा।।

अनुपल्लवि

चेडुकंटि रोग पीडितमै
चेडि वक्षीनिन्चे देहमु स्थिरमनि।। (एटुनम्मिनावो)

चरणं

मट्टिकूण्ड कन्टे हीनमैनदिदि।
माटि माटिकि रादु दीनिपै।
वट्टि मोहमु जेन्दुचुनु।
वरद वेंकटेश्वरूनि मरचि।। (एटुनम्मिनावो)

16. ENTANERCHINA

Ragam	: SAVERI — 15th Mayamalava Goula Janyam
Talam	: ADI
Arohanam	: S R_1 M_1 P D_1 $\dot{S}$
Avarohanam	: $\dot{S}$ N_3 D_1 P M_1 G_3 R_1 S
Pallavi	: Enta Nerchina Saphalamu Ēmi Endukee Chapalamu Ō Manasa
Anupallavi	: Santatambu Veda Sāstrādi Vara Sangeeta Sāhitya Vidya (lenta Nerchina)
Charanam	: Parakāya Pravesādi Tantramulu Paratatvādi Vedantamulu Dharalona Marigala Vidyalella Varada Venkateswaruni Kripaleka

16. एन्तनेर्चिन

राग : सावेरि
तालम् : आदि

पल्लवि

एन्तनेर्चिन सफलमु ऐमि।
एन्दुकी चपलमु ओ मनसा।।

अनुपल्लवि

सन्ततम्बु वेद शास्त्रादि वर।
संगीत साहित्य विद्य (लेन्तनेर्चिन)।।

चरणं

परकाय प्रवेशादि तंत्रमुलु।
परतत्वादि वेदान्तमुलु।
धरलोन मरिगल विद्यलेल्ल।
वरद वेंकटेश्वरुनि कृपलेक।।   (एन्तनेर्चिन)

17. INKA DAYA RĀLEDA

Ragam	: CHAKRAVAKAM – 16th Melakarta Ragam
Talam	: ADI
Arohanam	: S R_1 G_3 M_1 P D_2 N_2 $\dot{S}$
Avarohanam	: $\dot{S}$ N_2 D_2 P M_1 G_3 R_1 S
Pallavi	: Inka Daya Raleda Nāpai Inta Parānmukha Melanayya
Anupallavi	: Pankajāsanadyamara Vandita Pankeruhāksha Patita daitya Siksha
Charanam	: Santatambu Nee Satkathalanu vini Santoshamuga Bhajana Seyuchu Chinta Deerchi Nannu Brotuvani Nenento Pogadachundaga Itu Pantamela Jesevu Delupumu Patita pāvana Asrita Janaavana Dānta Varada Sri Venkatesa Dānavakula Srikara Bheekara

17. इंकदयरालेदा

राग : चक्रकाकम

तालम् : आदि

पल्लवि

इंकदयरालेदा नापै
इंतपरानमुख मेलनय्या।।

अनुपल्लवि

पंकजासनाद्यमर वन्दित
पंकेरूहाक्ष पतित दैत्य शिक्ष।।   (इंकदय)

चरणं

संततम्बु नी सत्कथलनु विनि।
संतोषमुगा भजन सेयुचु।
चिन्त दीर्चि नन्नु ब्रोतुवनि।
नेनेन्तो पोगडु चुण्डग इटु।
पंतमेल जेसेवु तेलुपुमु।
पतित पावन आश्रित जनावन।
दान्त वरद श्रीवेंकटेश।
दानवकुल श्रीकर भीकर।।   (इंकदय)

18. EPUDU KRIPA

Ragam : MUKHARI – 22nd Kharaharapriya Janyam
Talam : ADI
Arohanam : S R_2 M_1 P D_2 N_2 D_2 $\dot{S}$
Avarohanam : $\dot{S}$ N_2 D_2 P M_1 G_2 R_2 S
Pallavi : Epudu Kripa Kalguno Inakula Tilaka Neeku
Anupallavi : Ipudaina Kreeganta Jūsite Chālunani Enchi
Ninne Chāla Nammiyunna Nāpai

Charanam : Talli Tandri Anna Guru Daivamu Neeve yani
Dalachi Yevvaganaina Nannu Brotuvanuchu
Nā Yullamandu Chāla Nammika galavādai
Yunduterugavēmi Venkateswara Naapai

18. एपुड्डु कृप

राग : मुखारि
तालम् : आदि

पल्लवि

एपुड्डु कृप कलगुनो इनकुल तिलक नीकु।।

अनुपल्लवि

इपुडैन क्रीगंट जूसिते चालुननि
येन्चि निन्ने चाल नम्मियुन्न नापै।। (एपुड्डु कृप)

चरणं

तल्लि तन्ड्रि अन्न गुरु दैवमु नीवे यनि।
दलचि येव्वगनैन नन्नु ब्रोतुवनुचु।
ना युल्लमन्दु चाला नम्मिक गलवाडै।
युन्डुटेरुगवेमि वेंकटेश्वर नापै।। (एपुड्डु कृप)

19. KARUNINCHARA

Ragam : HUSSENI – 22nd Kharaharapriya Janyam
Talam : ADI
Arohanam : S R_2 G_2 M_1 P N_2 D_2 M_1 P N_2 D_2 N_2 $\dot{S}$
Avarohanam : S N_2 $\dot{S}$ P D_2 M_1 P M_1 G_2 R_2 S
Pallavi : Karuninchara Karunānidhe Sarivāralo chauka Seyakura

Anupallavi : Kari Rakshaka Kreeganta Jūdara Nannu
Parulevvaro Yani Enchakura

Charanam : Munu Prahlāduni Jūchi Chāla
Kanikarambutonu Kāpādinatlu
Nannu Kāchuta Nyāyamu gādā Ghanudau
Sri Venkatesanika

19. करूणिंचरा

राग : हुसेनि
तालम् : आदि

पल्लवि

करुणिंचरा करुणानिधे
सरिवारललो चौक सेयकूरा।।

अनुपल्लवि

करिरक्षक क्रीगन्ट जूडरा।
नन्नु परुलेव्वरो यनि एन्चकुरा।। (करुणिंचरा)

चरणं

मुनु प्रहलादुनि जूचि चाला।
कनिकरम्बुतोनु कापाडिनटुलु।
नन्नु काचुट न्यायमु गादा घनुडौ श्री वेंकटेशनिक।। (करुणिंचरा)

20. SANKALPAMETTIDO

Ragam : KHARAHARAPRIYA —
22nd Melakarta Ragam

Talam : ADI

Arohanam : S R_2 G_2 M_1 P D_2 N_2 $\dot{S}$

Avarohanam : $\dot{S}$ N_2 D_2 P M_1 G_2 R_2 S

Pallavi : Sankalpa mettido Manasā Sāketa Nilayadau
Rāmuni

Anupallavi : Pankeruhāsanadeenudaina Brahmakaina
Telusuno Teliyadō

Charanam : Sarvajeevānthakaranāseenudai
sarvakarmamulaku Sākshiyai yundi
Sarvaloka Niyamakudai Velayu
Sarvesudaina Venkatesuni

20. संकल्पमेट्टिदो

राग : खरहरप्रिय
तालम् : आदि

पल्लवि

संकलपमेट्ट्टिदो मनसा साकेत निलयुडौ रामुनि।

अनुपल्लवि

पंकेरूहासनादीनुडैन ब्रम्हकैन तेलुसुनो तेलियदो।। (संकल्पमेट्टिदो)

चरणं

सर्वजीवान्तकरणासीनुडै सर्व कर्ममुलकु साक्षियै युन्डि।
सर्वलोक नियमकुडै वेलयु।।
सर्वेसुडैन वेंकटेशुनि।। (संकल्पमेट्टिदो)

21. IDI NYĀYAMA

Ragam : MĀLAVI – 28th Harikambhoji Janyam
Talam : ADI
Arohanam : S R_2 G_3 M_1 P N_2 M_1 D_2 N_2 $\dot{S}$
Avarohanam : $\dot{S}$ N_2 D_2 N_2 P M_1 G_3 M_1 R_2 S
Pallavi : Idi Nyāyama Sri Rāmachandra Inchukaina
Daya leda Neevādanayya
Anupallavi : Sadayudaina chāla Nammitini Samayamide
Naapai Daya Ledā

Charanam : Ala yenuka Neekemi Tatana kotularedu
Neeto Buttena
Palurai Neekemi Etlaina Bāga delpavayya
Sri Venkatesa

21. इदि न्यायमा

राग : मालवि
तालम् : आदि

पल्लवि

इदि न्ययमा श्री रामचन्द्रा
इन्चुकैन दयलेदा नीवाडनय्या।।

अनुपल्लवि

सदयुडैन चाला नम्मितिनि
समयमिदे नापै दयलेदा।। (इदि न्यायमा)

चरणं

अल येनुक नीकेमि तटन
कोटुलरेडु नीतो बुट्टेना
पलुरै नीकेमि येटलैन बागा देलुपवय्या श्री वेंकटेश।। (इदि न्यायमा)

22. GARUDAGAMANA

Ragam : NAGASVARAVALI – 28th Harikambhoji Janyam
Talam : RUPAKAM
Arohanam : S G_3 M_1 P D_2 $\dot{S}$
Avarohanam : $\dot{S}$ D_2 P M_1 G_3 S
Pallavi : Gurudagamana Samayamide Karuna Jūda Radā

Anupallavi : Nirupama Sundaraakaara Nijabhakta Janaadhāra
Charanam : Pavanajaadi Nuta Dhrita Chapavanajaaptakulajaata
Pavanajaala Yādava Bhoopa Vanajaaksha Sri Venkatesa

22. गरुडगमन

राग : नागस्वरावलि
तालम् : रूपकं

पल्लवि

गरुडगमन समयमिदे करुण जूड रादा।।

अनुपल्लवि

निरुपम सुन्दराकारा निजभक्त जनाधारा।। (गरुडगमन)

चरणं

पवनजादिनुत ध्रित चपवनजाप्तकुलजात।
पवनजाल यादव भूप वनजाक्ष श्री वेंकटेश।। (गरुडगमन)

23. ENNADU DAYA

Ragam : BALAHAMSA – 28th Harikambhoji Janyam
Talam : RUPAKAM
Arohanam : S R_2 M_1 P D_2 Ṡ
Avarohanam : Ṡ N_2 D_2 P M_1 R_2 M_1 G_3 S
Pallavi : Ennadu Daya Vachchuno Inakula Tilaka
Anupallavi : Pannagasayana Naadu Paritapamulanu Teerchutaku

Charanam : Karimoralidagaane Vachchi Kanikaramuto
Brova Ledā
Dharabadi Hariyani Draupadini Brova Leda
Chira Jeevityadi Sakala Varamu losagu
Vāda vanuchu
Charanamulanu Neranammiti Varada
Venkateswara Neeku

23. एन्नडु दय

राग : बलहंस
तालम् : रूपकं

पल्लवि

एन्नडु दयवच्चुनो इनकुल तिलक।

अनुपल्लवि

पन्नगशयन नादु परितापमुलनु तींचुटकु।। (एन्नडु)

चरणं

करिमोरलिडगाने वच्चि कनिकरमुतो ब्रोवलेदा
दरबडि हरियनि द्रौपदिनि ब्रोवलेदा।
चिर जीवित्यादि सकल वरमुलोसगु वाडवनुचु।
चरणमुलनु नेर नम्मिति वरद वेंकटेश्वर नीकु।। (एन्नडु)

24. KANNA TANDRI NEEVE

Ragam : NARAYANI – 28th Harikambhoji Janyam
Talam : ADI
Arohanam : S R_2 M_1 P D_2 $\dot{S}$
Avarohanam : $\dot{S}$ N_2 D_2 P M_1 R_2 S
Pallavi : Kanna Tandri Neeve Ilāgu Nannu
Kadakandla Barachuta Nyāyama

Anupallavi : Sannutānga Sri Rāmachandra Naapai
Chalamela Ne Taala Jaalanayya

Charanam : Ishta Daivamu Neeve Analēda Kashtamella
Neeto Balkalēda
Santushtudai Ninne Koniyādaleda
Dushta Samhara Sri Venkateswara

24. कन्न तन्ड्रि नीवे

राग : नारायणि

तालम् : आदि

पल्लवि

कन्न तन्ड्रि नीवे इलागु नन्नु
कडकन्ड्ल बरचटु न्यायमा।।

अनुपल्लवि

सन्नुतांग श्री रामचन्द्र नापै
चलमेल ने ताल जालनय्य।। (कन्न तन्ड्रि)

चरणं

इष्ट दैवमु नीवे अनलेदा।
कष्टमुलेल्ल नीतो बलकलेदा।
संतुष्टुडै निन्ने कोनियाड लेदा।
दुष्ट संहार श्री वेंकटेश्वर।। (कन्न तन्ड्रि)

25. RAMA IKA NANNU

Ragam : SAHANA – 28th Ḥarikambhoji Janyam

Talam : RUPAKAM

Arohanam : S R_2 G_3 M_1 P M_1 D_2 N_2 $\dot{S}$

Avarohanam : $\dot{S}$ N_2 D_2 P M_1 G_3 M_1 R_2 G_3 R_2 S

Pallavi : Ramā Ika Nannu Brova Raada
Dayaleda Sri

Anupallavi : Tamasambu Jesite Ika Taalanu Parulanu
Vedanu

Charanam : Āaru Satruvulanu Batti Hatamu Jesi
Poorvarjita
Ghora Paapamulanu Pogotti Ne jesinatti
Neramulanu Manninchi Neeve Kaava
valenu Gaani
Verevarunnarura Sri Venkateswara
Dayākara

25. रामा इक नन्नु

राग : शहन
तालम् : रूपकं

पल्लवि

रामा इक नन्नु ब्रोव रादा
दयलेदा श्री।।

अनुपल्लवि

तामसम्बु जेसिते इक तालनु परुलनु वेडनु।। (राम इक)

चरणं

आरु शत्रुवुलनु बट्टि हतमु जेसि पूर्वार्जित।
घोर पापमुलनु पोगोट्टि ने जेसिनाट्टि।
नेरमुलनु मन्निन्चि नीवे काव वलेनु गानि।
वेरेवरुन्नारूरा श्री वेंकटेश्वर दयाकर।। (रामा इक)

26. NEJESINA NERAMU

Ragam : PURNACHANDRIKA – 29th Dheera Sankarabharana Janyam

Talam : ADI

Arohanam : S R_2 G_3 M_1 P D_2 P Ṡ

Avarohanam : Ṡ N_3 P M_1 R_2 G_3 M_1 R_2 S

Pallavi : Ne Jesina Neramu Littidani Neeve Naato Delpumu Rāma

Anupallavi : Sri Jaanaki Praana Naada Nee Chittamu Naa Bhagyamani Yunna

Charanam : Neevu gāka Vēru Daivamunnadani Nē Nenchi Ninnu Marachitina
Bhava Jana Sannuta Punya Naama Bhava Taaraka Sri Venkatesa

26. ने जेसिन नेरमु

राग : पूर्णचन्द्रिक
तालम् : आदि

पल्लवि

ने जेसिन नेरमु लिट्टिदनि
नीवे नातो देलपुमु रामा।।

अनुपल्लवि

श्री जानकी प्राण नाथा
नी चित्तमु ना भाग्यमनि युन्न।। (ने जेसिन)

चरणं

नीवु गाक वेरु दैवमुन्नदनि
ने नेन्चि निन्नु मरचितिना
भाव जन सन्नुत पुण्य नाम
भव तारक श्री वेंकटेश।। (ने जेसिन)

27. NINNU JUCHI

Ragam	: SAURASHTRAM – 17th Surya Kanta Janyam
Talam	: ADI
Arohanam	: S R_1 G_3 M_1 P M_1 D_2 N_3 Ṡ
Avarohanam	: Ṡ N_3 D_2 N_2 D_2 P M_1 G_3 M_1 G_3 R_1 S
Pallavi	: Ninnu juchi Dhanyudaiti Neeraja Netra
Anupallavi	: Vanajaasanaadi Vandita Charana Vanajanaabha Devaadi Deva
Charanam	: Sakala Lokaadhaara Sachchidaakaara Sakala Jeeveswara Sarveswara Sakala Varadaayaka Sree Venkateswara

27. निन्नुजूचि

राग : सौराष्ट्रम

तालम् : आदि

पल्लवि

निन्नुजूचि धन्युडैति नीरज नेत्र।

अनुपल्लवि

वनजासनादि वन्दित चरण।
वनजनाभ देवादि देव।। (निन्नुजूचि)

चरणं

सकल लोकाधारा सच्चिदाकारा।
सकल जीवेश्वर सर्वेश्वर।
सकल वरदायक श्री वेंकटेश्वर।। (निन्नुजूचि)

28. NEE PAADAMULE GATIYANI

Ragam : BHAIRAVI – 20th Natabhiravi Janyam

Talam : ADI

Arohanam : S R_2 G_2 M_1 P D_2 N_2 $\dot{S}$

Avarohanam : $\dot{S}$ N_2 D_1 P M_1 G_2 R_2 S

Pallavi : Nee Paadamule Gatiyani Nammiti
Neerajakshi Parāshakti

Anupallavi : Sri Panchanadeeswaruni Rāni
Srita Jana Paalini Dharma Samvardhini

Charanam : Kaamita Phala Dāyaki Kaumāri
Kaama Dahanuni Manohari Sankari
O! Mahakāli Sanāthani Omkaara sadani
Bhavāni
Saamaja Samāgamani Sukha Bhāshini
Sakala Loka Janani Paapa Samani
Paamara Asura Mada Bhanjani Paraatpari
Bhavāni Niranjani

28. नीपादमुले गतियनि

राग : भैरवि

तालम् : आदि

पल्लवि

नीपादुमुले गतियनि नम्मिति
नीरजाक्षि पराशक्ति।।

अनुपल्लवि

श्री पंचनदीश्वरुनि राणि।
श्रितजन पालिनि धर्म संवर्धनि।। (नीपादमुले)

चरणं

कामित फलदायकि कौमारि।
काम दहननि मनोहरि शंकरि।
ओ! म[illegible] [illegible]ातनि ओम्कार सदनि भवानि।
सामज श[illegible] सुख भाषिणि।
सकल लोक जननि पाप शमनि।
पामर असुर मद भन्जनि
परात्परि भवानि निरन्जनि।। (नीपादमुले)

29. VARUMULOSAGI

Ragam	: KEERAVANI — 21st Melakarta Ragam
Talam	: RUPAKAM
Arohanam	: S R_2 G_2 M_1 P D_1 N_3 $\dot{S}$
Avarohanam	: $\dot{S}$ N_3 D_1 P M_1 G_2 R_2 S
Pallavi	: Varamu Losagi Brochuta Neekaruda Jagadaadhāra
Anupallavi	: Parama Dayakara Suguna Varada Ne Korina
Charanam	: Udara Poshanaardhamai Orula Manasu Karaga Balkinadi Oka Bhārata mouna Tudanu Sukhamu Gaanaka Ne Madini Chinta Nonduchu Vēmari Neeto Telipitiga Madana Janaka Venatesa Manasu Neeku Kaligiyunte

29. वरमुलोसगि

राग : कीरवाणि

तालम् : रूपकं

पल्लवि

वरमुलोसगि ब्रोचुट नीकरूदा जगदाधार।।

अनुपल्लवि

परम दुयाकर सुगुण वरदा ने कोरिन।। (वरमुलोसगि)

चरणं

उदर पोषणार्धमै ओरूल मनसु करग
बल्किनदि ओक भारत मौना
तुद्नु सुखमु गानक
ने मदिनि चिन्त नोन्दुचु
वेमरि नीतो तेल्पितिगा
मदन जनक वेंकटेश
मनसु नीकु कलिगियुंटे।। (वरमुलोसगि)

30. KARUNINCHUTA KIDE

Ragam : SINDHU MANDĀRI –
29th Dheera Sankarabharana Janyam
Talam : ADI
Arohanam : S R_2 G_3 M_1 P Ṡ
Avarohanam : Ṡ N_3 D_2 P G_3 M_1 D_2 P M_1 R_2 S
Pallavi : Karuninchuta kide Samayamayya
Kari Rakshaka Nākali Deerchavayya
Anupallavi : Dharalo Nee Vanti Daivamu Ledani
Paramaanandamuto Bhajiyinchitini
Charanam : Kamalaasanaadi Sannuta Paada
Kamaneeya Sukha Shyamala Gaatra
Kamalaa Kalatra Kanja dala Netra
Amaraadi Posha Adi Venkatesa

30. करुणिंचुट किदे

राग : सिन्धुमन्दारि

तालम् : आदि

पल्लवि

करूणिंचुट किदे समयमय्या।
करिरक्षक ना आकलि दीर्चवय्या।।

अनुपल्लवि

धरलो नीवन्टि दैवमु लेदनि।
परमानन्दमुतो भजिइंचितिनि।। (करूणिंचुट किदे)

चरणं

कमलासनादि सन्नुत पादा।
कमनीय सुख श्यामल गात्रा।
कमला कलत्र कंजदल नेत्र।
अमरादि पोष आदि वेंकटेश।। (करूणिंचुट किदे)

31. INTAKANTE KAAVALENA

Ragam : KANNADA – 29th Dheera Sankarabharana Janyam
Talam : RUPAKAM
Arohanam : S M_1 G_3 M_1 P M_1 D_2 N_3 $\dot{S}$
Avarohanam : $\dot{S}$ N_3 $\dot{S}$ D_2 P M_1 G_3 M_1 R_2 S
Pallavi : Inta kante Kaavalena Ī Kashtamu Chālada Rāma
Anupallavi : Suntainanu Naa Manasuku Sukhamu Leka Jesitivi Gaada
Charanam : Puttina Naadanunde Ī Pottasāgute Paniga

Petti Nalugurilo Naadu Guttu Bayalu Jesitivi
Itti Gunamu Galavaadani Gattiga
Ne TelusuKonti
Vatti Maataletiki Sri Varada Venkateswara

31. इन्तकंटे कावलेना

राग : कन्नड़
तालम् : रूपकं

पल्लवि

इन्तकंटे कावलेना ई कष्टमु चालदा रामा।।

अनुपल्लवि

सुन्तैननु ना मनसुकु
सुखमु लेक जेसितिवि गादा।। (इन्तकंटे)

चरणं

पुट्टिन नाड नुन्डे ई पोट्टसागुटे पनिगा।
पेट्टि नलुगुरिलो नादु गुट्टु बयलु प्जेसितिवि।
इट्टि गुणमु गलवाडनि
गट्टिग ने तेलुसुकोंटि
वट्टि माटलोटिकि श्री
वरद वेंकटेश्वर।। (इन्तकंटे)

32. RGHUVAMSA SUDHAMBUDHI

Ragam : KADANAKUTHUHALAM – 28th Kambhoji Janyam
Talam : ADI
Arohanam : S R_2 M_1 D_2 N_2 G_3 P $\dot{S}$
Avarohanam : $\dot{S}$ N_2 D_2 P M_1 G_3 R_2 S

Pallavi : Raghuvamsa Sudhāmbudhi Chandra Sri
Rāma Raaja Rājeswara

Anupallavi : Agha Megha Māruta Srikara Asuresa
Mrigendra Dhara Jagannādha

Charanam : Bhrugunandana Garvabhanjana Brindāraka
Brindahita Kadanaa-
Nigamaantavaasamudaavanaa Neerjaksha
Venkateswara

32. रघुवंश सुधाम्बुधि

राग : कदनकुतूहलम

तालम् : आदि

पल्लवि

रघुवंशसुधाम्बुधि चन्द्र श्री राम राज राजेश्वरा

अनुपल्लवि

अघ मेघ मारुत श्रीकर असुरेश
मृगेन्द्र धर जगन्नाथ।। (रघुवंश सुधाम्बुधि)

चरणं

भ्रगुनन्दन गर्वभंजन ब्रिन्दारक बिन्दहित कदना।
निगमान्तवासमुदावना नीरजाक्ष वेंकटेश्वर।। (रघुवंश सुधाम्बुधि)

33. MANSUKARUGADEMI

Ragam : HAMSADHWANI –
29th Dheera Sankarabharana Janyam

Talam : RUPAKAM

Arohanam : S R_2 G_3 P N_3 Ṡ

Avarohanam : Ṡ N_3 P G_3 R_2 S

Pallavi : Manasu Karugademi Sri Māninee Manohara Nee

Anupallavi : Vanajabhavādi Vinuta Geervānaadula Brochina Nee

Charanam : Aramara Etiki Nee Kula Birudunu Dalachi Chūdumu
Saranamanina Degakai Tana Sareeramunu Kosichchina
Karunākarudagu sibi Bhūvarudu Needu Taata Gadaa?
Marachitivo Emō Sri Varada Venkateswara Nee

33. मनसुकरुगदेमि

राग : हंसध्वनि

तालम् : रूपकं

पल्लवि

मनसुकरुगदेमि श्री मनिनी मनोहर नी।।

अनुपल्लवि

वनजभवादि विनुत गीर्वाणादुल ब्रोंचिन नी।। (मनसुकरुगदेमि)

चरणं

अरमर एटिकि नी कुल बिरुदुनु दलचि चूडुमु
शरणमनिन डेगकै तन शरीरमुनु कोसिच्चिन
करुणाकरुडगु सिबि भूवरुडु नीदु तात गदा
मरचितिवो एमो श्रीवरद वेंकटेश्वर नी।। (मनसुकरुगदेमि)

34. PARIDĀNAMICHCHITE

Ragam : BILAHARI — 29th Dheera Sankarabharana Janyam
Talam : KHANDA JHAMPE
Arohanam : S R_2 G_3 P D_2 Ṡ
Avarohanam : Ṡ N_3 D_2 P M_1 G_3 R_2 S
Pallavi : Paridaanamichchite Pālintuvemo
Anupallavi : Paramapurusha Sripati Naapai Neeku
Karunakalgakayunna kaaraṇamemayya
Charanam : Rokkamichchutaku Nē Mukkanti Cheli Gaanu
Chakkani Chelini Yosaga janaka Raajunu Gaanu
Mikkili Sainyamivva Mārkatendrudu Gaanu
Ākkatika Metugalgu Adi Venkatesa Neeku

34. परिदानमिच्चिते

राग : बिलहरि
तालम् : खंड चापु

पल्लवि

परिदानामच्चिते पालिन्तुवेमो।।

अनुपल्लवि

परमपुरुष श्रीपति नापै नीकु
करुण कल्गकयुन्न कारणमेमय्या।। (परिदानमिच्चिते)

चरणं

रोक्कमिच्चुटकु ने मुककंटि चेलिगानु
चक्कनि चेलिनियोसग जनक राजुनु गानु
मिक्किलि सैन्यमिव्व मार्कटेन्द्रुडु गानु
आक्कटिक मिटुगल्गु आदि वेंकटेश नीकु।। (परिदानमिच्चिते)

35. ABHIMĀNAMENNADU

Ragam	: BEGADA – 29th Dheera Sankarabharana Janyam
Talam	: ADI
Arohanam	: S G_3 R_2 G_3 M_1 P D_2 N_3 D_2 P $\dot{S}$
Avarohanam	: $\dot{S}$ N_3 D_2 P M_1 G_3 R_2 S
Pallavi	: Abhimaanamennadu kalgu Rāma Amarendra Vandita Paada Naapai
Anupallavi	: Ibha Rāja Varadaa Naapai Nee Kinta Kopamelanayya Nee Vaadani
Charanam	: Anna Vastramula Kemidovayani Yennadaina Ninnu Adiginaana Kanna Tandri Neeveyani Nammi Nee Karuna Galgite Chālunani Yundaga Tinnagaanu neevu Vidanaada Jūchite Nannu Brochevaarevarayya Vennudaina Sri Venkatesa Naadu Vinnapapambu Vinaraada Naato Vaada

35. अभिमानमेन्नडु

राग : बेगडा

तालम् : आदि

पल्लवि

अभिमानमेन्नडु कल्गु रामा
अमरेन्द्र वन्दित पाद नापै।।

अनुपल्लवि

इभ राज वरदा नापै नीकिन्त
कोपमेलनय्या नी वाडनि।। (अभिमानमेन्नडु)

चरणं

अन्न वस्त्रमुल केमिदोवयनि
एन्नडैन निन्नु अडिगिनाना
कन्न तंड्रि नीवेयनि नम्मि नी
करुण गल्गिते चालुननि युन्डग
तिन्नगानु नीवु विडनाड जूचिते
नन्नु ब्रोचेवारेवरय्या
वेन्नुडैन श्री वेंकटेश नादु
विन्नपम्बु विनरादा नातो वादा।। (अभिमानमेन्नडु)

36. MANASUNANERA

Ragam : BEGADA — 29th Dheera Sankarabharaṅa Janyam
Talam : RUPAKAM
Arohanam : S G_3 R_2 G_3 M_1 P D_2 N_3 D_2 P $\dot{S}$
Avarohanam : $\dot{S}$ N_3 D_2 P M_1 G_3 R_2 S
Pallavi : Manasuna Nera Nammiti Ni Mahimalu Vini Ne Satatamu
Anupallavi : Anaga Nannetlaina Aadarinchi Brotuvanuchu
Charanam : Krurudaina Kaakasurudu Kori saranamanaga Natani
Kroora Krityamulaku Neeve Kopimpaka Kāsinatula
Neramento Ne Jesinanu Nannu Mannintuvanuchu
Varanārada Harana Sri Varada Venkatesa Anuchu

36. मनसुन नेर

राग : बेगडा

तालम् : रूपकं

पल्लवि

मनसुन नेर नम्मिति नी महिमलु विनि ने सततमु।।

अनुपल्लवि

अनघ नन्नेट्लैन आदरिन्चि ब्रोतुवनुचु।। (मनसुन नेर)

चरणं

क्रूरूडैन काकासुरुडु कोरि शरणमनग नतनि
क्रूर कृत्यमुलगु नीवे कोपिम्पक काचिनटुल
नेरमेन्तो ने जेसिननु नन्नु मन्निन्तुवनुचु
वारणार्ति हरण श्री वरद वेंकटेश अनुचु।। (मनसुन नेर)

37. NINNUJEPPA

Ragam	: MANDĀRI – 51st Kamavardhini Janyam
Talam	: ADI
Arohanam	: S R_1 G_3 M_2 P N_3 $\dot{S}$
Avarohanam	: $\dot{S}$ N_3 P M_2 G_3 R_1 S
Pallavi	: Ninnu Jeppa Kaaranamemi Manasa Munu Ne Jesina Karma Mitlundaga
Anupallavi	: Tanayādi Tana Paasa Bhaktudai Ghanamaina Paamarudainanduku
Charanam	: Palumaaru Durbhāshiyai Tirigi Kulaheenamaina Krutyamul Salpuchu Kalalonanaina Sri Venkatesayani Dalachaleni Paapa Krutyudainanduku

37. निन्नुजेप्प

राग : मन्दारि
तालम् : आदि

पल्लवि

निन्नुजेप्प कारणमेमि मनसा
मुनु ने जेसिन कर्मम् इट्लुंडग।।

अनुपल्लवि

तनयादि तन पाश भक्तुडै
घनमैन पामरुडैनन्दुकु।। (निन्नु जेप्प)

चरणं

पलुमारु दुर्भाषियै तिरिगि
कुलहीनमैन कृत्यमुलु सल्पुचु
कललोननैन श्री वेंकटेशयनि
दलचलेनि पाप कृत्युडैनन्दुकु।। (निन्नु जेप्प)

38. ENDUKITU

Ragam : MANDĀRI – 51st Kamavardhini Janyam
Talam : MISRA CHAPU
Arohanam : S R_1 G_3 M_2 P N_3 $\dot{S}$
Avarohanam : $\dot{S}$ N_3 P M_2 G_3 R_1 S
Pallavi : endukitu Chapalamu Anave Manasa
Ikanaina Telusu Kommanave
Anupallavi : Indu Dharudani Daamodarudani
Peredukoni Yunna Vaadokkadani Enchaka
Charanam : Parama Bhāgavatula Hridayamuna Vasinchi
Vaaru Korina
Niravadhi Sukhamu Lichchuvaadani
Varada Venkateswaruni Smarinchaka

38. ऐन्दुकिटु चपलमु

राग : मन्दारि
तालम् : मिश्रचापु

पल्लवि

ऐन्दुकिटु चपलमु अनवे मनसा
इकनैन तेलुसु कोम्मनवे।।

अनुपल्लवि

इन्दु धरूडनि दामोदरुडनि
पेरेडुकोनि युन्न वाडोक्कडनि एंचक।। (एन्दुकिटु)

चरणं

परम भागवतुल हृदयमुन वसिंचि वारु कोरिन।
निरवधि सुखमु लिच्चुवाडनि।
वरद वेंकटेश्वरूनि स्मरिंचक।। (एन्दुकिटु)

39. KORINAVARAMOSAGU

Ragam : RAMAPRIYA – 52nd Melakarta Ragam
Talam : RUPAKAM
Arohanam : S R_1 G_3 M_2 P D_2 N_2 $\dot{S}$
Avarohanam : $\dot{S}$ N_2 D_2 P M_2 G_3 R_1 S
Pallavi : Korina Varamosagu mayya Kōdanda Paani
Anupallavi : Vaarijastra Janaka Sri Vatsānga Nishkalanka
Charanam : Sarivaarilona Nannu Sauka Jeyavaladu Needu
Marapujochchiyunna Nannu Maanamuto
Kaapaadumu
Parichara Vaanara Samooha Paapa Dahana
Vaari Vaaha
Karirāja Varada Venkateswara Muraari
Kaada

39. कोरिन वरमोसगु

राग : रामप्रिय

तालम् : रूपकं

पल्लवि

कोरिन वरमोसगु मय्य कोदन्ड पाणि।।

अनुपल्लवि

वारिजास्त्र जनक श्री वत्सांग निष्कलंक।। (कोरिन वरमोसगु)

चरणं

सरिवारिलोन नन्नु सौक जेयवलदु नीदु।
मरपुजोच्चि युन्न नन्नु मानमुतो कापाडुमु।
परिचर वानर समूह पाप दहन वारि वाह।
करि राज वरद वेंकटेश्वर मुरारि कादा। (कोरिन वरमोसगु)

40. ITTIVARU LETIKI

Ragam : RAMAPRIYA – 52nd Melakarta Ragam
Talam : ADI
Arohanam : S R_1 G_3 M_2 P D_2 N_2 $\dot{S}$
Avarohanam : $\dot{S}$ N_2 D_2 P M_2 G_3 R_1 S
Pallavi : Itti Vaaru Lētiki Butterayya Īlaagu Baruvai Gudiki Chedai
Anupallavi : Puttu Chaavu Lēni Atti Taavu Gani Pattalēka Mada Brashtulai Tirigi
Charanam : Paradravya Apahaarulai Vishayatrulai Smarakinkarulai Iha Paramettidani Erugaleka Sri Varada Venkateswaruni Marache

40. इट्टिवारू लेटिकि

राग : रामप्रिय
तालम् : आदि

पल्लवि

इट्टिवारू लेटिकि बुट्टेरय्या
ईलागु बरूवै गुडिकि चेडै।।

अनुपल्लवि

पुट्टु चावु लेनि अट्टि तावु गनि
पट्टलेक मद भ्रष्टुलै तिरिगि।। (इट्टिवारु लेटिकि)

चरणं

परद्रव्य अपहारूलै विषयत्रुलै स्मरकिंकरूलै
इह परमेट्टिदनि एरुगलेक श्री वरद
वेंकटेश्वरूनि मरचे।। (इट्टिवारू लेटिकि)

41. VARAMEEYAVAYYA

Ragam : SUDDHA DHANYASI –
22nd Kharaharapriya Janyam
Talam : ADI
Arohanam : S G_2 M_1 P N_2 $\dot{S}$
Avarohanam : $\dot{S}$ N_2 P M_1 G_2 S
Pallavi : Varameeyavayya Dharanaayaka
Anupallavi : Saratindu Sekharamitra Sridhara Paapahara
Sara Chaapa Kara
Charanam : 1. Paramaarthakamaina Panulella Maani
Ghoramaina Paapa
Krutyamulu Salpuchu Varagaana Jaarulai
Tirige Saara Heenulanu Sannuti Seyani
(Varameeya Vayya)

2. Vara Naaradaadi Sūryaksha Kinnarulu
   Nerchina
   Vara Sangeeta Swara
   Saukhyamulerugaleni
   Dhara Nara Jeevulanu Smariyinchani
   (Varameeya Vayya)

3. Purushottama Sri Varada Venkatesa
   Karunā Katāksha Kari-
   –Rakshaka Sri Hari Hari Hari Yani
   Santatamu Sthira
   Chittamuto Bhajiyinchedi
   (Varameeya Vayya)

41. वरमीयवय्या

राग : शुद्धधन्यासि

तालम् : आदि

पल्लवि

वरमीयवय्या धरनायक।।

अनुपल्लवि

शरदिन्दु शेखरमित्र श्रीधर पापहर शर
चाप कर।। (वरमीयवय्या)

चरणं

1. परमार्थकमैन पनुलेल्ल मानि।
   घोरमैन पाप कृत्यमुलु सल्पुचु।
   वरगान जारुलै तिरिगे।
   सारहीनुलनु सन्नुति सेयनि।। (वरमीयवय्या)
2. वर नारदादि सुरयक्ष किन्नरुलु नेर्चिन।
   वर संगीत स्वर सौख्यमुलेरुगलेनि।
   धर नर जीवुलनु स्मरियिंचनि।। (वरमीयवय्या)

3. पुरुषोत्तमा श्री वरद वेंकटेश
करुणा कटाक्ष करि रक्षक
श्री हरि हरि हरि यनि
संततमु स्थिर चित्तमुतो भजियिंचेडि।। (वरमीयवय्या)

42. MARIVEREDIKKEVARAYYA

Ragam : SHANMUKHAPRIYA – 56th Melakarta Ragam
Talam : ADI
Arohanam : S R_2 G_2 M_2 P D_1 N_2 $\dot{S}$
Avarohanam : $\dot{S}$ N_2 D_1 P M_2 G_2 R_2 S
Pallavi : Marivere Dikkevarayya Raama Maati Maatikini Telupavalenaa
Anupallavi : Daridaapulēni Naa Jaali Deerchi Daya chesi Broche Dora Neevu Kaada
Charanam : Ninnu Chaala Nammi Yunna Vaadanuchu Nee Chittamunake Telisiyundaga Sannutaanga Sri Venkatesa Neevu Nannu Brovaka Yunduta Nyāyamā

42. मरिवेरे दिक्केवरय्या

राग : षन्मुखप्रिय
तालम् : आदि

पल्लवि

मरिवेरे दिक्केवरय्य रामा।
माटि माटिकिनि तेलुपवलेना।।

अनुपल्लवि

दरि दापु लेनि ना जालि दीर्चि।
दय जेसि ब्रोचे दोर नीवु कादा।। (मरिवेरे दिक्केवरय्या)

चरणं

निन्नु चाल नम्मि युन्न वाडनुचु
नी चित्तमुनके तेलिसियुंडग
सन्नुतांग श्री वेंकटेश नीवु
नन्नु ब्रोवक युंडुट न्यायमा।। (मरिवेरे दिक्केवरय्या)

43. APARĀTHAMULANNIYU

Ragam : LATANGI — 63rd Melakarta Ragam
Talam : ADI
Arohanam : S R_2 G_3 M_2 P D_1 N_3 $\dot{S}$
Avarohanam : $\dot{S}$ N_3 D_1 P M_2 G_3 R_2 S
Pallavi : Aparāthamulanniyu Manninchi
Ādarimpumayya Ne Jēsina
Anupallavi : Kripajēsi Nā Manavyalakinchi
Kreeganta Jūda Samayamide
Charanam : Vēga Nannu Brovumani Ninnu Ento
Vēdukontinayya Sri Venkatesa Itu
Jāgu Seyaka Nā Veta Dālakane
Jāli Chendi Nannu Brovakunna Nā

43. अपराधमुलन्नियु

राग : लतांगि
तालम् : आदि

पल्लवि

अपराधमुलन्नियु मन्निंचि
आदरिंचुमय्य ने जेसिन।।

अनुपल्लवि

कृपजेसि ना मनवियालकिंचि।
क्रीगन्ट जूड समयमिदे।। (अपराधमुलन्नियु)

चरणं

वेग नन्नु ब्रोवुमनि निन्नु एन्तो
वेडुकोन्टिनय्य श्री वेंकटेश इटु।
जागु सेयक ना वेतदालकने
जालि जेंदि नन्नु ब्रोवकुन्न ना।। (अपराधमुलन्नियु)

44. NIJADASĀVARADA

Ragam	: KALYANI – 65th Melakarta Ragam
Talam	: ADI
Arohanam	: S R_2 G_3 M_2 P D_2 N_3 $\dot{S}$
Avarohanam	: $\dot{S}$ N_3 D_2 P M_2 G_3 R_2 S
Pallavi	: Nija Daasa Varada Akhila Jagadaananda
Anupallavi	: Bhujagaadhipa Sayana Bhoomijaa Ramana Aja Purandaraadi Vinuta Sukhyaata
Charanam	: Kaushika Yaagaari Taatakaadi Samharana Gautama Sati Saapa Megha Sameerana Isha Kodanda Khandana Dhureena Ina Vamsaja Sree Venkatesa

44. निजदास वरदा

राग : कल्याणि
तालम् : आदि

पल्लवि

निजदास वरदा अखिल जगदानन्द।

अनुपल्लवि

भुजगाधिप शयन भूमिजा रमणा
अज पुरंदरादि विनुत सुख्यात।। (निजदास वरदा)

चरणं

कौशिक याग ताटकादि संहरण।
गौतम सति शाप मेघ समीरण।
ईश कोदन्ड कन्दन धुरीण।
इन वंशज श्री वेंकटेश।। (निजदास वरदा)

45. Ā SAMYAMUNA

Ragam : SĀRANGA — 65th Mechakalyani Janyam
Talam : ADI
Arohanam : S R_2 S P M_2 G_3 M_2 P D_2 N_3 Ṡ
Avarohanam : Ṡ D_2 P M_2 R_2 G_3 M_1 R_2 S
Pallavi : Ā Samayamuna Kēmi Dalachina Chesitivi
Ō Manasa
Anupallavi : Ī Samayamuna Nunde Impu Sompu Juchi
Valachute Naadu Sarikaadaniyunde
Charanam : Ore Ore Dhushta Jeevudayanuchu
Ugramaina Ghōshamuto Biluchuchu
Ghora Roopamukha Yamudu Bhādhalato
Gūdi Vachchi Eduta Nilichi Vēgame
Raayanuchu batti Gatti Gottuchu
Krūrudai Himsalanu Jeyu Vēla
Ore Varada Venkatesayani
Oka Saranuni Biluvalēka Potivi

45. आ समयमुन

राग : सारंग
तालम् : आदि

पल्लवि

आ समयमुन केमि दलचिन
चेसितिवि ओ मनसा।।

अनुपल्लवि

ई समयमुन नुन्डे इम्पु सोम्पु जूचि
वलचुटे नाडु सरिकादनि युन्डे।। (आ समयमुन)

चरणं

ओरे ओरे दुष्ठ जीवुडयनुचु
उग्रमैन घोषमुतो बिलुचुचु
घोर रुपमुख यमुडु बाधलतो
गूडि वच्चि एदुट निलचि वेगमे।
रायनुचु बट्टि गट्टि गोट्टुचु।
क्रूरुडै हिंसलनु जेयु वेल।
ओरे वरद वेंकटेशयनि
ओक शरनुनि बिलुवलेक पोतिवि।। (आ समयमुन)

46. MANASĀ VRUDHA

Ragam : ABHOGI – 22nd Kharaharapriya Janyam
Talam : ADI
Arohanam : S R_2 G_2 M_1 D_2 $\dot{S}$
Avarohanam : $\dot{S}$ D_2 M_1 G_2 R_2 S
Pallavi : Manasā Vrudha garva mētike
Maharāju Laina Manujule Gadā
Anupallavi : Manasāra Sākshuni Kripaleka
Mana Sāmardhya Mēmunnadi
Charanam : Mana Sāhasa Yuddhamu Jeya Nantha
Mana Sādhyamu Lēdani Pāndavulu
Manasāra Venkatesa Charanamana
Sāradhiyai Vachchi Brovalēdā

46. मनसावृधा

राग : अभोगि
तालम : आदि

पल्लवि

मनसा वृधा गर्व मेटिके
महराजुलैन मनुजुले गदा।।

अनुपल्लवि

मनसार साक्षुनि कृपलेक
मन सार्मध्यमेमुन्नादि।। (मनसा वृधा)

चरणं

मन साहस युध्द्मु जेय नंत
मन साध्यमु लेदनि पांडवुलु
मनसार वेंकटेश शरणमन
सारधियै वच्चि ब्रोवलेदा।। (मनसा वृधा)

47. SARASEERUHĀNANA

Ragam : BRINDAVANASARANGA — 22nd Kharaharapriya Janyam
Talam : ADI
Arohanam : $S\ R_2\ M_1\ P\ N_2\ \dot{S}$
Avarohanam : $\dot{S}\ N_2\ P\ M_1\ R_2\ G_2\ S$
Pallavi : Saraseeruhānana Sree Rāma
Anupallavi : Dharaja Manohara Sankha Chakra Dheera
Sree Kara Dānava Hara
Charanam : Vāsavādi Poojita Vara Charana
Vaaranarthi Bhanjana Nipuna Karuna
Vasudeva Padmanābha Suresa Varada
Venkatesa Sarvesa

47. सरसीरुहानन

राग : बृन्दावनसारंग
तालम् : आदि

पल्लवि

सरसीरुहानन श्री रामा।।

अनुपल्लवि

धरजा मनोहर शंख चक्र धर
श्रीकर दानव हर।। (सरसीरुहानन)

चरणं

वासवादि पूजित वर चरण
वारणार्ति भंजन निपुण करुण
वासुदेव पद्मनाभ सुरेश वरदा
वेंकटेश सर्वेश।। (सरसीरुहानन)

48. DHANYUDEVVADO

Ragam : MALAYAMARUTAM — 16th Chakravaka Janyam
Arohanam : S R_1 G_3 P D_2 N_2 $\dot{S}$
Avarohanam : $\dot{S}$ N_2 D_2 P G_3 R_1 S
Pallavi : Dhanyudevvado Dāsaradhe
Anupallavi : Anyamandu Chittamandiyyaka
Brahmānandāmruta Pānamu Jēsē
Charanam : Vara Maddela Tālādi Tambura
Veena Vādyamula Jerchukoni
Swara Suddhamuto Sukhamu
Sree Varada Venkateswaruni Bhajinche

48. धन्युडेव्वडो

राग : मलयमारुतम
तालम् : आदि

पल्लवि

धन्युडेव्वडो दाशरथे।।

अनुपल्लवि

अन्यमन्दु चित्तमंदिय्यक
भ्रम्हानंदामृत पानमु जेसे।। (धन्युडेव्वडो)

चरणं

वर मद्दल तालादि तंबुर
वीणा वाद्यमुल जेंचुकोनि
स्वर शुधमुतो सुखमु
श्री वरद वेंकटेश्वरुनि भजिंन्चे।। (धनयुडेव्वडो)

(*Note*: Some musicians feel that the above composition is a Kriti of "Manambu-Chavadi Venkatasubbayyar but it has gained popularity mainly as Patnam Subramanya Iyer's composition.)

10

Jāvalis of Patnam Subramanya Iyer

(Lyrics Only)

1. KANUGONTINI

Ragam : DESIYA TODI – 8th Hanumathodi Janyam

Talam : ADI

Arohanam : S G_2 M_1 D_1 N_2 $\dot{S}$

Avarohanam : $\dot{S}$ N_2 D_1 P M_1 G_2 R_1 S

Pallavi : Kanugontini Tētadellamika Kaligiro Vāni Marmamittidani

Anupallavi : Vinave Aluvagaladi Bhōdhanaku Lobadiyunna Atadini

Charanam :
1. Mātaladelpute Maguvaro NātoMārubalka Yunnādemoyani Yunti
   Matimātiki Podinintanundi Chedi Indu Vachchi Chūse Jādalache
2. Virahadala Taapamu Taalaka
   Nāyuramu cherchi Kaugalinchukontini
   Taruni Nannu koodani Venkateswarudu
   Apudanu Konna Mātalache

1. कनुगोंटिनि

राग : देशीय तोडि
तालम् : आदि

पल्लवि

कनुगोंटिनि तेटदेल्लमिक
कलिगिरो वानि मर्ममिट्टिदनि

अनुपल्लवि

विनवे अलु वगलाडि बोधनकु
लोबडियुन्न अतडिनि।। (कनुगोंटिनि)

चरणं

1. माटलाड पोते मगुवरो नातो
मारुबल्क युन्नदेमोयनि युन्टि
माटि माटिकि पोदिनिन्ट नुन्डि
चेडि इन्दु वच्चि चुसे जाडलचे।। (कनुगोन्टिनि)

2. विरहानल तापमु तालक
नायुरमु चेर्चि कौगलिन्चिुकोन्टिनि
तरुणि नन्नु कूडनि वेंकटेश्वरुड
पुडनु कोन्न माटलचे।। (कनुगोन्टिनि)

2. APUDU MANASU

Ragam : KHAMAS — 28th Harikambhoji Janyam
Talam : RUPAKAM
Arohanam : S M_1 G_3 M_1 P D_2 N_2 $\dot{S}$
Avarohanam : $\dot{S}$ N_2 D_2 P M_1 G_3 R_2 S
Pallavi : Apudu Manasu Niluchunate
Ativaro Idētimātalapudu
Anupallavi : Chapalameti kituvanti Sāmarthyamu
Galavādaina

Charanam : 1. Chokkapu Yauvanamugala Chakkani
Purushudu Yuvatula
Pakka jēri Sarasamuga Balkuchu
Kanusaiga Jēyaga
2. Varada Venkateswaruditu Suratikēli
Salpakōrina
Tarunamulo Marudu virisaramula
Birabira Kuriyaga (Apudu Manasu)

2. अपुडु मनसु

राग : खमास
तालम् : रूपकं

पल्लवि

अपुडु मनसु निलुचुनटे
अतिवरो इदेटिमाटलेपुडु

अनुपल्लवि

चपलमेटि किटुवन्टि सामर्थयमु गलवाडैन।। (अपुडु मनसु)

चरणं

1. चोक्कपु यौवनमु गल
चक्कनि पुरुषुडु युवतुल
पक्कजेरि सरसमुगा
बल्कुचु कनुसैग जेयग।। (अपुडु मनसु)

2. वरद वेंकटेश्वरुडिटु
सुरतिकेलि सल्पकोरिन
तरुणमुलो मरुडु विरिशरमुल
बिरबिर कुरियग।। (अपुडु मनसु)

3. MARIYĀDA TELIYAKANE

Ragam : SURATI — 28th Harikambhoji Janyam
Talam : RUPAKAM
Arohanam : S R_2 M_1 P N_2 $\dot{S}$ N_2 D_2 N_2 $\dot{S}$
Avarohanam : $\dot{S}$ N_2 D_2 P M_1 G_3 P M_1 R_2 S
Pallavi : Mariyāda Teliyakane Mātalāduta Tagunate
Anupallavi : Parihāsamu Jeyatagina Varusa Kaligiyunte Nēmi
Charanam :

1. Sarasa Sallāpamulaku Samayamu Kāgāde Ēmo
   Sarasijākshi Nāvanti Satulu Gumpu Gūdiyundaga (Mariyāda)
2. Veladirō Nannu Gūdinatlu Venkateswarudu Neepai
   Balavantamuga Nēnu Valachi Vachchina Nemi (Mariyāda)

3. मरियाद तेलियकने

राग : सुरटि
तालम : रूपकं

पल्लवि

मरियाद तेलियकने माटलाडुट तगुनटे

अनुपल्लवि

परिहासमु जेयतगिन वरुस कलिगियुन्टेनेमि।। (मरियाद)

चरणं

1. सरस सल्लापमुलकु समयमु कागादे एमो।
   सरसिजाक्षि नावन्टि सतुलु गुम्पु गूडियुन्डग।। (मरियाद)

2. वेलदिरो नन्नु गूडिनटुलु
वेंकटेश्वरुडु नीपै बलवंतमुगा
नेनु वलचि वच्चिन नेमि।। (मरियाद)

4. SAMYAMIDE RĀRĀ

Ragam	: BEHAG – 29th Dheera Sankarabharana Janyam
Talam	: RUPAKAM
Arohanam	: S G_3 M_1 P N_3 D_2 N_3 $\dot{S}$
Avarohanam	: $\dot{S}$ N_3 D_2 P M_2 G_3 M_1 G_3 R_2 S
Pallavi	: Samayamide Rāra Nāsāmi Tāmasinchakura
Anupallavi	: Kamala Vairi Chanu Tenchina Kānksha Leederādura
Charanam	:1. Magadu Ūraledu Nā Māma gāri Jōli Lēdani Vagadega Telisinadiga Vatti Pantamēlarā (Samayamide)
	2. Mannanache Neevu Vachchi Nannu Gūdi Yundinatlu Ninna Rēyi Kalakanti Neerajaksha Venkatesa (Samayamide)

4. समयमिदे रारा

राग : बेहाग
तालम् : रूपकं

पल्लवि

समयमिदे रारा ना सामि तामसिंचकुरा।।

अनुपल्लवि

कमल वैरि चनु तेन्चिन कांक्ष लीडेरादुरा।। (समयमिदे)

चरणं

1. मगडु ऊरलेडु ना माम गारि जोलि लेदनि।
   वगडेग तेलिसिनदिगा वट्टि पंतमेलरा।। (समयमिदे)

2. मन्ननचे नीवु वच्चि नन्नु गूडि युंडिनटुलु
   निन्न रेई कलकंटि नीरजाक्ष वेंकटेश।। (समयमिदे)

5. VADDANI NE NANTINIGA

Ragam : KAPI — 22nd Kharaharapriya Janyam
Talam : RUPAKAM
Arohanam : S R_2 M_1 P N_2 Ṡ
Avarohanam : Ṡ N_2 D_2 N_2 P M_1 G_2 R_2 S
Pallavi : Vaddani Ne Nantiniga
Vāni Joli Neeku Cheli
Anupallavi : Suddha Mosagādane Vā-devatano
Jerināde (Vaddani Ne Nantiniga)
Charanam : Chokkapu Doravalenu Chāla
Vakkanagā Mātalāduchu
Nakka Vinayamunu Jēse
Takkarito Sahavāsamu
(Vaddani Ne Nantiniga)

5. वद्दनि ने नन्टिनिगा

राग : कापि
तालम् : रूपकं

पल्लवि

वद्दनि ने नन्टिनिगा
वानि जोलि नीकु चेलि।।

अनुपल्लवि

शुध्द मोसगाडने वा
डेवतनो जेरिनाडे।। (वद्दनि ने नन्टिनिगा)

चरणं

चोक्कपु दोरवलेनु चाला
वक्कनगा माटलाडुचु
नक्क विनयमुनु जेसे
टक्करितो सहवासमु।। (वद्दनि ने नन्टिनिगा)

❋❋❋

11

Tillana of Patnam Subramanya Iyer

(Lyrics with Notation)

THADHEEM DHEEMTHA NANA

Ragam	: PHARAJ – 15th Mayamalava Goula Janyam
Talam	: ADI
Arohanam	: S M_1 G_3 M_1 D_1 M_1 D_1 N_3 $\dot{S}$
Avarohanam	: $\dot{S}$ N_3 D_1 P M_1 G_3 R_1 S
Pallavi	: Thadheem dheem thatananam Tom Tadara Takitadheem Tarikitathaka ThākitaKitathaka Thakatharikitathaka
Anupallavi	: Nādaradheem Nādaradheem Thadiyanare Dheemtha Thajenu Thakadheentha Thaka Jhanu Thakadheentha Thakathari Kitathaka Thaddhithalanguthom Thakadhi thalanguthom Thakathari Ginathom
Charanam	: Sudathi Neeku Tagina Chinnadira Surati Kelikadi Balu Sūtira Sadayudaina Venkateswara Ninu Saraguna Rammanera Samayamura

तधीमधीमत नन

राग : फ़रज़
तालम् : आदि

पल्लवि

तधीम धीमत तननम तोमतदर
तकिटधीम तरिकिटतक ताकिटकिटतक
तकतरि किटतक।। (तधीम धीमत)

अनुपल्लवि

नादरधीम नादरधीम तदियनरे धीमत
तदरदानि तोमन्द्रु दानि तिरुनादर दरधीम
नझेणु तकधीम ततकझेणु तकधीम
तत्कतरि-किटतक,
तदित्तलांन्गुतोम तकदित्तन्लांगुतोम
तकतरि गिणतोम।। (तधीम धीमत)

चरणं

सुदति नीकु तगिन चिन्नदिरा
सुरति केलिकदि बलुसूटिरा
सदयुडैन वेंकटेश्वर निनु
सरगुन रम्मनेरा समयमुरा।। (तधीम धीमत)

Pallavi 8×4 = 32

S , N , , , D , , , P ,– D , M , |
Tha– Dheem – – Dheem – – Tha– Tha– na –

G , , , , ,– M G | M , D ,– D , N , ||
Nam– – – – – Thom – – Tha– da – ra –

D , P , M , G , , ,– G M G R S Ṇ |
Tha– ki – ta – Dheem – – Thari ki ta Thaka

S MGM– DMDN I Ṡ NDM– DMDN II
Tha– ki ta Ki ta thaka Thaka thari Ki ta thaka
(Tha Dheem)

Anupallavi

D , DD D , , ,– N , NN N , , , I
Na– da ra Dheem– – Na– da ra Dheem– –

Ṡ , Ṡ , Ṙ , Ṡ , I N ,– Ṡ , , , Ṡ , II
Tha– di – ya – na – Re – Dheem – – Tha–

Ṡ , Ṅ , Ṡ , Ġ–, , , Ġ ,– Ṁ , Ġ , I
Tha– da – ra – Da– – – ni – Thom dri–

Ṙ Ṡ , – Ṡ , N , I Ṡ , ND– DMD , II
Dani – – Thi– ru – Nā– da ra da ra Dheem

M , MM– GMD , , , N , NNMD I
Tha– Jhenu Thaka Dheem – – Tha– thaka Jhenu

MDN , , , N , I Ṡ ND M– GMDN II
Thaka Dheem – – Tha– Thaka Thari ki ta Thaka

N Ṡ Ġ , Ṡ Ṙ , N Ṡ , , , MDN , I
Tha– Dhi– thalān gu Thom– – Thaka Dhee

D N , M D , , , I N D M M GMDN II
Thalan ku Thom– – Thaka Thari Gi na Thom
(Tha Dheem)

Charanam

Ṡ , N , D , P , , , M , G , M , I
Su – da – Thi– Nee– – – ku – Tha– gi –

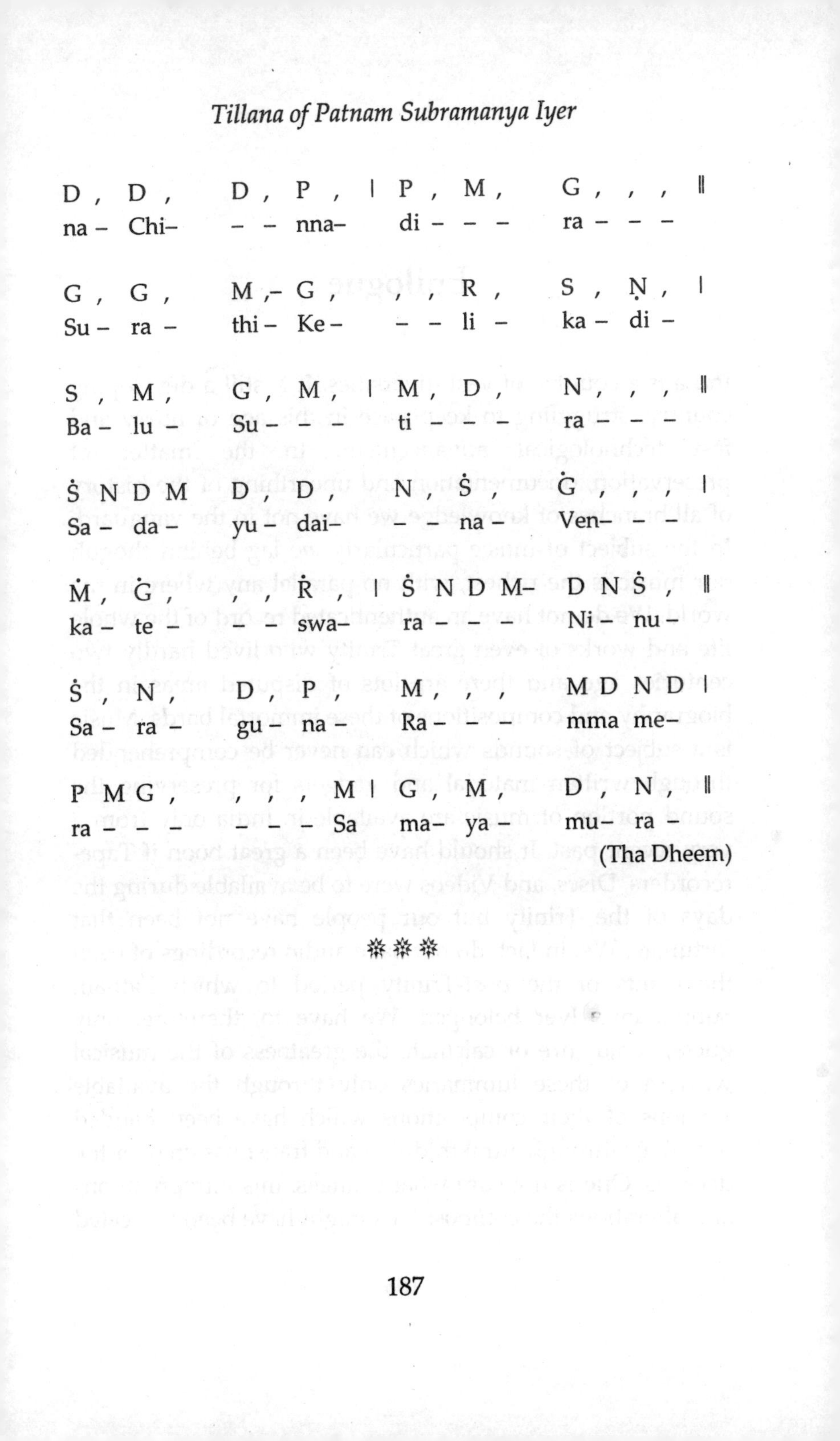

D , D , D , P , | P , M , G , , , ||
na – Chi– – – nna– di – – – ra – – –

G , G , M ,– G , , , R , S , Ṇ , |
Su – ra – thi – Ke – – – li – ka – di –

S , M , G , M , | M , D , N , , , ||
Ba – lu – Su – – – ti – – – ra – – –

Ṡ N D M D , D , N , Ṡ , Ġ , , , |
Sa – da – yu – dai– – – na – Ven– – –

Ṁ , Ġ , , , Ṙ , | Ṡ N D M– D N Ṡ , ||
ka – te – – – swa– ra – – – Ni – nu –

Ṡ , N , D , P , M , , , M D N D |
Sa – ra – gu – na – Ra – – – mma me–

P M G , , , , M | G , M , D , N , ||
ra – – – – – – Sa ma– ya – mu– ra –
(Tha Dheem)

❋❋❋

Epilogue

India is a country of vast diversities. It is still a developing country, struggling to keep pace in this age of hurry and fast technological advancement. In the matter of preservation, documentation and unearthing of the history of all branches of knowledge we have not in the vanguard. In the subject of music particularly we lag behind thoguh our music is the richest, with no parallel any where in the world. We do not have an authenticated record of the whole life and works of even great Trinity who lived hardly two centuries ago and there are lots of disputed areas in the biography and compositions of these immortal bards. Music is a subject of sounds which can never be comprehended through written material and gadgets for preserving the sound portion of music are available in India only from a very recent past. It should have been a great boon if Tape-recorders, Discs, and Videos were to be available during the days of the Trinity but our people have not been that fortunate. We, in fact, do not have audio recordings of even the giants of the post-Trinity period to which Patnam Subramanya Iyer belonged. We have to, therefore, only guess, conjucture or calculate the greatness of the musical wisdom of these luminaries only through the available versions of their compositions which have been handed over to us through aural tradition and transmission over the decades. One is not sure what changes, mis-intrepretations and alterations the compositions might have been subjected to while passing through generations of learners and teachers. With regards to biographical details reliance upon here says is still not totally avoidable. The custom of incorporating some miracle or other in the lives of great composers was in vogue even up to this century. Biographies of the post-Trinity luminaries are comparatively free from mystifying accounts but exaggerated versions of anecdotes relating to their musical achievements continue to exist.

In the midst of such abstract and unspecified availability of information, it is a rather tough and challenging job to prepare a comprehensive and exhaustive monograph of any one perpersonality of Patnam Subramanya Iyer's period. The informations dealt with in this humble work is far from exhaustive. The approach has thus been more musical than musicological.

***